CHASING THEIR DREAMS

Chinese Settlement in the
Northwest Region of British Columbia

BY LILY CHOW

Chasing Their Dreams
©2000 Lily Chow

Caitlin Press Inc.
Box 2387 Station B
Prince George BC V2N 2S6

Book design and Cover by Denis & Muntener Advertising Ltd.
Photos supplied from author's personal collection and the B.C. Archives
Index by Katherine Plett

Canadian Cataloguing in Publication Data

Chow, Lily, 1931-
  Chasing their dreams

  Includes index
  ISBN 0-920576-83-4

  1. Chinese--British Columbia, Northern--History. 2. Chinese Canadians--British Columbia,Northern--History, 3. British Columbia, Northern--Race relations. I. Title,
FC3850.C5C55 2000   971.1'8004951   C00-910963-3
F1089.7.C5C41 2000

Caitlin Press acknowledges the financial support of Canada Council for the Arts for our publishing program. Similarly we acknowledge the support of the Arts Council of British Columbia.

Cover Photo Credits:
Top: Harry Chow smoking a traditional Chinese water pipe. *Photo courtesy Harry Low*
Bottom: Cook Lee Yet Fee at the Red Rose Mine in the Hazelton area circa 1939. *Photo courtesy Bill McRae*

CONTENTS

ACKNOWLEDGMENT

First and foremost, I would like to thank the Canadian Heritage Department, Multiculturalism and Citizenship Canada for funding the research of this writing project. Without their financial assistance, it would have been impossible to carry out all my research in the various places of the Skeena-Bulkley Valley. I am truly indebted to Mr. Douglas Findlater, the senior program officer, who supported this writing project and encouraged me to continue with the research on the Chinese settlement in this province. His belief in this project gave me the opportunity to discover some Chinese Canadian history previously unknown.

Now I wish to express my sincere gratitude to Dr. Robin Fisher, Ron Hatch, Anita Olsen, Cynthia Wilson, Francis Wong, and Jim Wong-Chu for their letters of support; Kaori Donovan, a graduate student of UNBC, for helping me in gathering data from Statistics Canada and locating articles from newspapers. I would like to thank my very good friends, Bobbie Suen and Dr. Fleming McConnell who spent time to proof read the manuscripts and offered suggestions to make this writing more refined. Also, thank you to my editors, Cynthia Wilson, Candice Dyck, Frank White and Patricia Tourand.

To Pat McCammon in Smithers, Francis Wong in Prince Rupert, and Anthony Yao in Kitimat, I offer my sincere appreciation for leading me to meet with some key members in their communities. Without their assistance I would not have been able to collect some of the most vital information in this book.

I'll never forget the day when Francis took me to visit the North Pacific Cannery Museum Village. Although it was in winter, the cloudy sky and the freezing rain could not dampen his thoughtful spirit to assist me. It was off-season for visitors, but Herb Pond, the manager of the Cannery Museum, opened the doors and took me on a tour. He patiently explained to me the functions of the various kinds of nets for commercial fishing and allowed Francis and I to take photographs in the Cannery Museum. When I visited the Cannery Museum again in 1998, David Boyce opened the doors of some displayed cabinets for me to take photographs of various artifacts. In Prince Rupert I met Gladys Blyth, who was very knowledgeable about the history of many fish canneries at the mouth of the Skeena River; she shared with me extensive information about the fish canning process in the early days. Anthony Yao and Gina Cheng, too, supplied many photographs for this book. To these wonderful people, I offer my heartfelt thanks.

Since most of the Chinese communities in the Skeena-Bulkley Valleys are relatively small, and many Chinese senior members have left the areas, tracing the history of Chinese settlement in these areas became a challenge. Not many records about the lives of the early Chinese immigrants were found. Fortunately, many kind Canadians generously shared with me their memories of early Chinese immigrants. They are Diane Smith in Atlin; Sylvia Cotton, Jessie Gould, Eric Janze, Charlotte Sullivan and Ward Marshall in Hazelton; Eleanor Kedell and Louis Shaw in Kitimat; Jim Martin and Barbara Sheppard in Prince Rupert; Floyd Frank, Mamie Kirkby, Bill and Helene McRae and Yvonne Moen in Terrace; Vera Heggie, Gordon Hetherington, Ruby Hoskins, Chuck Morris, Maudye Peterson, Daintree Riffel, Wilf Watson, Lillian Weedmark and Gordon Williams in Smithers, and Dr. Eldon Lee in Prince George. Their recollections about Chinese Canadians and immigrants in their areas have added many interesting anecdotes to this book. My very special thanks to all of them.

I would also like to express my sincere appreciation to the following friends. They are Hing Mung, the President of Alcan Asia Ltd., in Hong Kong; Greg and Anna Chan, and Tim Leong in Hazelton; Daphne Cai, Harry Cheng, Francis Huen, Tung-Hoi and Winne Lai, Kin Ming Lo, Bill Mah, Tam Ka Chung, Anita Tam, and Zhang He in Kitimat; Charlotte Jang, Jerry Jang, Michelle Lai, Gordon Lam, Danny Mah, Pat Mah, Amy S. Wong, Francis Wong and Horne Wong in Prince Rupert; Ken Kwan and Jim Woo in Smithers; Sam and Susie Locke, and Glenn Wong in Terrace. Last but not least, I like to extend my gratitude to Eugene, Carminah and Sandy Calisto for providing accommodation while I was in Terrace, and Anthonio and Maria Figueiredo for their kind hospitality.

Now credits to the following institutions: The British Columbia Provincial Archives, Victoria; Special Collections, University of British Columbia; Bulkley Valley Historical and Museum Society; Hazelton Pioneer Museum and Archives; Kitimat Centennial Museum; Smithers Museum, Prince Rupert City and Regional Archives; Prince Rupert Fire Department and the Prince George Public Library.

Lily Chow

FOREWORD

Lily Chow has provided a missing link in the Canadian history in her writing. The narrative of the early Chinese and their contributions to the building of this country will certainly diminish the arrogant self-righteousness of the Canadian majority, especially those in the past. The Chinese came to Canada for reasons not too dissimilar to other settlers, yet they have often been suspected, historically, on other unfounded grounds. The description of the Klondike saga is indeed incredible. It exposed the injustice of an elected municipal Government, for a democracy without justice is worse than benevolent authoritarianism.

Lily does justice not only to the history of Chinese in British Columbia but also to the greater context of the history of the oppressed people. Her writing represents a lonely voice crying out for justice and denouncing hypocrisy. She writes with depth of research and lucidity of language the epic of early Chinese in the northwest of British Columbia.

This book is morally challenging and thought provoking to anyone concerned with minority immigration to Canada. It is an indelible part of Canadian history.

Dr. W. C. Tan
President,
Canadian College for Chinese Studies
Victoria, BC

MAP OF THE SKEENA-
BULKLEY VALLEY

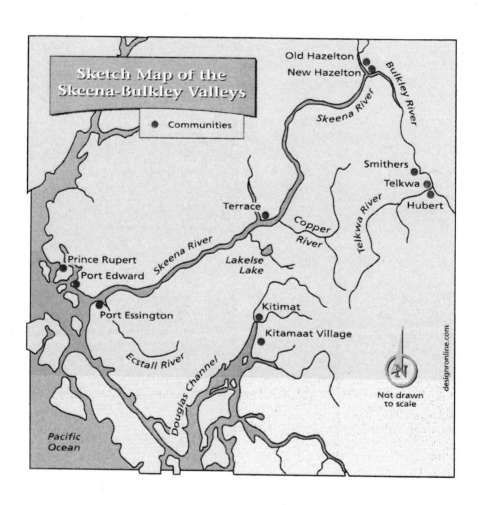

Sketch Map of the
Skeena-Bulkley Valleys

Communities

Old Hazelton
New Hazelton
Bulkley River
Skeena River
Smithers
Telkwa
Hubert
Telkwa River
Terrace
Copper River
Prince Rupert
Port Edward
Skeena River
Lakelse Lake
Port Essington
Kitimat
Kitamaat Village
Ecstall River
Douglas Channel
N
Not drawn
to scale
designronline.com
Pacific
Ocean

MAP OF HAZELTON
& VICINITY

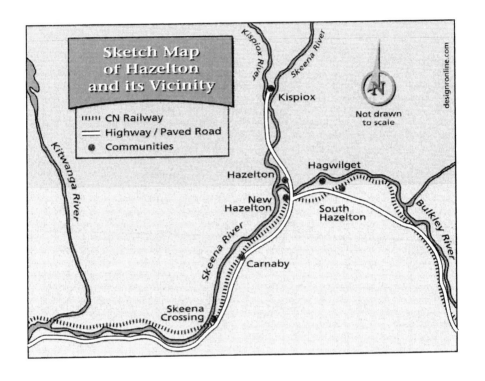

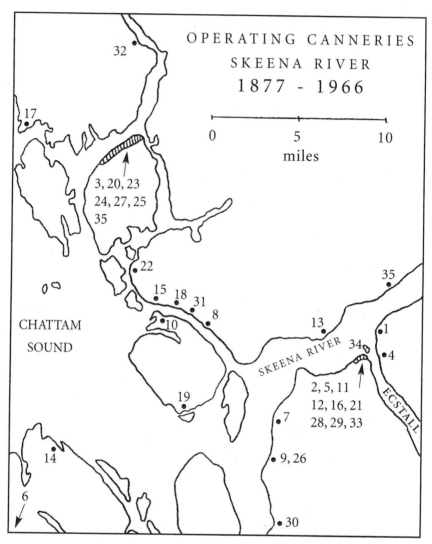

OPERATING CANNERIES
SKEENA RIVER
1877 - 1966

32

17

3, 20, 23
24, 27, 25
35

0   5   10
miles

35

22

15 18 31
         8

CHATTAM
SOUND

10

13

1

SKEENA RIVER   34

4

2, 5, 11
12, 16, 21
28, 29, 33

ECSTALL

19

7

14

9, 26

6

30

CANNERY	FIRST OPERATED	CANNERY	FIRST OPERATED	CANNERY	FIRST OPERATED
1. Alexandria	1904	14. Humpback Bay	1929	25. Royal	1959
2. Anglo-alliance	1899	15. Inverness	1876	26. Royal Canadian	1892
3. Babcook	1957	16. Ladysmith	1901	27. Seal Cove	1943
4. Balmoral	1883	17. Metlakatla	1882	28. Skeena or	
5. British America	1883	18. North Pacific	1889	Cunningham	1883
6. Captain Cove	1926	19. Oceanic	1903	29. Skeena River	
7. Carlisle	1895	20. Oceanside	1951	Commercial	1902
8. Cassiar	1903	21. Pearce	1902	30. Standard	1890
9. Claxton	1898	22. Port Edward	1918	31. Sunnyside	1916
10. Dominion	1906	23. Prince Rupert	1940	32. Tuck's Inlet	1913
11. Globe	1899	(Nelson Brothers)		33. Turnbull's	1902
12. Herman's	1901	24. Prince Rupert	1962	34. Village Island	1906
13. Haysport	1920	Co-op		35. Windsor	1878

MAP OF THE CASSIAR
REGION

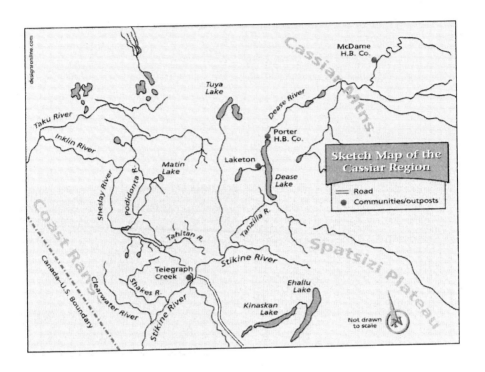

MAP OF CHINA

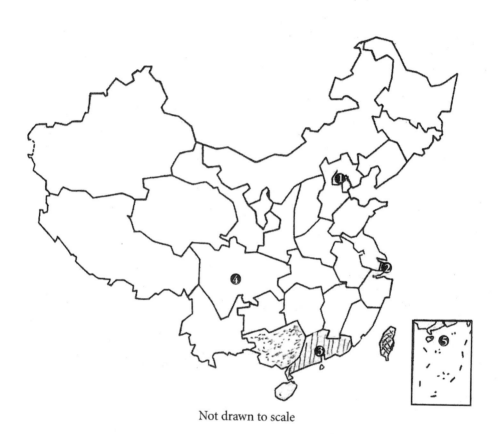

Not drawn to scale

LEGEND:

(1) Beijing
(2) Shanghai
(3) Guangzhou
(4) Chongqing
(5) Hong Kong

 Guangdong

 Guangxi

 Taiwan

MAP OF KITIMAT

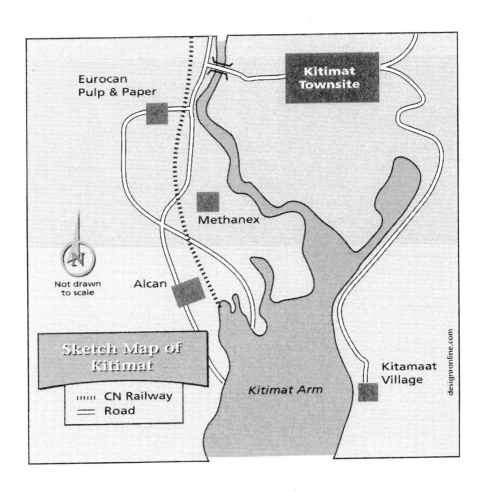

Eurocan
Pulp & Paper

Kitimat
Townsite

Methanex

Not drawn
to scale

Alcan

Kitamaat
Village

Kitimat Arm

Sketch Map of
Kitimat

||||| CN Railway
═══ Road

designronline.com

INTRODUCTION

A few years ago, I was invited to a party by a group of Japanese friends. It was held at Chee Duck Tong, a Chinese community building in Prince George. At the party, I met a young Chinese engineer who had arrived in town not too long ago. While he looked around at the building he exclaimed, "I didn't know there was a Chinese organization in this city!"

I was not at all surprised to hear such a remark. Many people, including myself when I first arrived in Canada, did not realize that a large number of Chinese immigrants had reached the Interior of British Columbia (BC) in the past one hundred and fifty years.

My intent is to describe the Chinese Canadian settlements in the Skeena and Bulkley Valleys and in the Cassiar region. For readers' convenience, I would like to define certain terms used throughout this book. These terms are used to identify the Chinese settlers who came to this province during the different periods of time, and those who were born here. Generally, the expression "Chinese Canadians" refers to all the Chinese settlers who have acquired Canadian citizenship. The phrase "Chinese immigrants" refers to landed immigrants who have not yet become Canadian citizens and to all the Chinese old-timers who came to this country prior to 1948. The early Chinese immigrants, especially those in BC, were not recognized as Canadian citizens until after World War II. Finally, the term "Canadian-born Chinese" is self-explanatory, referring to those Canadians with Chinese ancestry.

Before exploring the Chinese settlements, I would like to present some of the reasons why the early Chinese people left their homeland and came to British Columbia. All the Chinese immigrants, in the past or present, came to Canada to find better lives. The definition of a better life for the early Chinese immigrants was relatively simple; they just dreamed of finding the essentials–food, clothing and shelter–for themselves and their family members.

In the nineteenth century, the Qing Government of China was weak and corrupt. They were incompetent in dealing with the intrusions of western powers or to restrain the threats of invasion from Japan. After the two Opium Wars–in 1840-1842 and 1856-1860–China was forced to sign the Nanking Treaty and then the Tianjing Treaty with Britain, hence allowing foreigners to occupy some Chinese territories. For example, a certain part of Shanghai became an English concession while another area within the city became a French concession. In these enclaves the Chinese Government could not exercise its own laws. China also had to open its ports for western trade and pay huge indemnities to Britain.[1] This led to heavy taxation for the Chinese. The majority of the common folk, especially the peasants, were already living in starvation and poverty. Many peasants did not own land, but rented their farm from landlords who required them to pay a large rental fee, either in the form of goods or silver. Arable land was rare, and the country was overpopulated. The production of crops was insufficient to support the population growth. Droughts, floods and attacks by locusts frequently caused crop failures. Thefts, robberies, violence and assaults were common occurrences in many villages. Obviously, the Chinese people were struggling to make ends meet; living between deep sea and hell fire. Under such oppressive and difficult conditions, some impoverished peasants often took up arms and rebelled against the Qing Government. In 1850, the Taiping Rebellion, one of the peasant uprisings, set out to destroy the Qing regime, but was defeated in 1864.

In 1894, Japan invaded Manchuria, the northeast region of China and the home of the Qing people. After the defeat in the Sino-Japanese War in 1895, China was profoundly humiliated because it had to give Japan Taiwan and its territory in Liaodong Peninsula. Again, it had to pay its eastern neighbor a massive indemnity. All these disastrous and disgraceful events stimulated a nationalism movement in the country, and a number of revolutionary parties were formed with the intention of overthrowing the Qing Government. Having witnessed the failures of many past insurrections, and having lived in hardship and suffering for so long, many Chinese people could not see the light at the end of the tunnel. They looked for opportunities to leave the country, at least temporarily, hoping that they could find better lives for themselves and provide means to improve the living conditions of their families. Hence, in the nineteenth century, the miserable situation in China motivated many people to leave the country.

Meanwhile, gold was being discovered in British Columbia. A large number of Chinese people from the delta of the Pearl River (Zhu Jiang) were lured to this province, then a British colony, to find the yellow treasure. According to some senior Chinese Canadians, their grandfathers who ventured to BC wrote home that gold was literally visible in the lower Fraser River and its tributaries. Thus many Chinese people came and followed the white miners to climb over mountains and walk through swamps in the wilderness looking for the yellow treasure. As more people penetrated into the Interior, roads had to be built for transporting provisions and equipment to the miners. The first wagon road between Harrison and Lillooet was built in 1858, followed by the construction of another which connected Yale to the Cariboo around 1860. Many Chinese immigrants were engaged in the construction of these wagon roads as well as assisting in the building of bridges across rivers and streams in mining areas. Between 1880 and 1885 it was estimated that about 15,000 Chinese labourers were being employed in the construction of CPR.[2] The opportunities of finding wealth in gold mining and employment in road and railway construction were attractive to the Chinese immigrants. These opportunities also provided them with hope of achieving their dreams of finding the essentials of life, as well as realizing their visions for a better future, not only for themselves but for their children and other family members.

Unfortunately, the path leading to the realization of their hopes and dreams was challenging. Besides living in a cold and harsh physical environment, and enduring loneliness and isolation, they were confronted with prejudice and discrimination. When the economy of this country was good, the presence of the Chinese immigrants was generally ignored or tolerated. As the economy slowed down after the exhaustion of gold in the Fraser Valley, the Chinese miners were treated like aliens, and hostility began to surface. The Chinese settlers were disenfranchised in 1875.

Meanwhile, many white miners moved to the Cariboo area, believing that the mother lode was imbedded somewhere in the North. They attempted to prevent Chinese miners from following them but were not successful. When the Chinese miners eventually reached the Cariboo gold fields, they were often accused of not applying for a mining license and of not paying dues.[3] Early news reports, documents, and writings often labeled the Chinese immigrants as "Chinamen," "Celestials," "Mongolians," "heathens," "barbarians" and other derogatory terms. They were often despised, rejected, and condemned.

After the completion of the CPR, many Chinese labourers were left stranded. The CPR Company and the contractors, who brought them over, made no attempt to compensate them or help them to go home. Ultimately, the Chinese labourers took up any jobs that were available and were willing to work for less than other workers did. Their survival strategies did not bring about any appreciation or understanding among the whites. Instead, the immigrants were accused of taking jobs away, and the anti-Chinese movement began. Their rights were stripped away and they were not allowed to acquire any Crown land after 1884. Many anti-Chinese organizations were formed, especially in the lower mainland.

The motives of these organizations were to prevent the Chinese immigrants from getting into the job market and, if possible, to expel them from the province. They made attempts to stop public works, industries and businesses from employing Chinese labourers. They held public meetings and accused the immigrants of doing wrong. Their allegations included the beliefs that the Chinese immigrants came here with no intention of making this country their home; that they supported no churches and charitable institutions, that they didn't take any interest in the advancement of the province, and so on[4]. These anti-Chinese organizations passed resolutions to get rid of the Chinese and sent petitions to the Dominion Government to make their concerns and desires known.

The anti-Chinese movement led to the formation of two Royal Commissions, one in 1885 and the other in 1904, to study the Chinese issues. In 1885, the Chinese Restriction Act was passed, and the head tax of $50.00 was introduced. Chinese immigrants had to pay the head tax before being let in to Canada as an attempt to discourage their immigration. The exceptions were merchants, their wives and children; consular officers, their families and servants; clergymen, their wives and children; students who intended to enter degree-conferring universities, and teachers and men of science.[5] When the Restriction Act failed to deter the Chinese people from coming, more anti-Chinese agitation took place. In 1901 the head tax was increased to $100, and in 1904 to $500. As a result, most of the Chinese immigrants who came to this country after 1904 were single men because they simply could not afford to bring their families with them.

The conditions in China did not encourage the stranded labourers to go home either. After the formation of the Chinese Republic in 1912, the country still remained in a state of chaos and unrest. The Republican Government initiated the Northern Expedition, a military strategy to get rid of the warlords. Shortly after, civil war between the Guomindang and the Communist party began. Adding to all of this, the threat of Japanese invasion still haunted the country. All these factors triggered more Chinese people to leave. Many borrowed money to pay for the head tax to gain entry to Canada, thus increasing the Chinese population in British Columbia despite the head tax.

This phenomenon caused even greater alarm among the white Canadians.

Finally, the anti-Chinese organizations managed to convince the Dominion Government to stop Chinese immigration. In 1923 the infamous Chinese Exclusion Act was passed to prohibit Chinese entry to this country, except for those belonging to the categories mentioned in the Chinese Restriction Act. The Chinese settlers had to register with the immigration department every six months. This policy also included their Canadian-born children. Many senior Canadian-born Chinese still possesses the registration documents with the statement saying "the bearer is not a Canadian citizen." For this reason all the early Chinese settlers and their Canadian-born children can be referred to as Chinese immigrants. Many would have left Canada if they could have afforded to buy their passage home. They had no choice but to settle in this country and find some means to keep alive. Making their lives harder, the BC Government policy officially denied employment to the Chinese. In order to protect themselves, they formed organizations and clan associations to help and support one another. They segregated themselves and lived apart from the white society, thus creating the many Chinatowns in the province.

Since they could not find employment readily, they turned to market gardening and set up small businesses such as laundries, restaurants, bakeries, general, and grocery stores. They took up work as domestic servants in private homes and as cooks in sawmills and railroad camps. Some enterprises, such as the construction of the Grand Trunk Pacific Railway (GTP) and mining companies in remote areas were allowed to employ Chinese labourers when they could not find any white labourers to take the jobs. Many fish canneries were also permitted to employ Chinese workers to perform messy jobs like cleaning and gutting fish, which white men often refused to do. These were the only exceptions in the anti-Chinese policy of Vancouver Trades and Labour Council which spearheaded the anti-Chinese labour practices.

The fish industries along the Pacific north coast and at the mouth of the Skeena River attracted a large number of Chinese workers to the North as early as 1876 when the Inverness Cannery, the first fish cannery on the north coast of BC was established. The Chinese were seasonal workers who migrated to the north coast during salmon runs and returned to the lower mainland when the canning season was over. Some of them eventually settled in Prince Rupert and vicinity during the construction of the Grand Trunk Pacific Railway. In 1906 when Prince Rupert was selected as the terminus for the Grand Trunk Pacific Railway, president Charles M. Hays, wanted not only to develop Prince Rupert as a port and railway terminus, but also to create a modern metropolitan city comparable to New York or San Francisco. Hays' plan motivated many people, including some Chinese immigrants, to move north to find employment, to set up businesses and to speculate on land. Many Chinese people went to Prince Rupert to start small businesses. Some contracted work from the GTP to manufacture railroad ties and to supply other building materials for the railway company.

A few Chinese immigrants did very well in their businesses. Their success stories motivated more Chinese to emigrate from China and provided hope for those who lived in this province. So, they held on to their dreams that one day they could improve the lives of their families in China. Like their predecessors, some of these successful Chinese immigrants provided assistance to their relatives and friends to immigrate to Canada until the Exclusion Act was enforced in 1923. This kind of "chain sponsorship," a common pattern among the Chinese immigrants, resumed again after 1948 when the Immigration Act was modified to allow more Chinese people to immigrate to this country.

After World War II (WWII), the Federal Government made a series of modifications in the Immigration Act. These changes resulted from the appeals for justice and humanitarianism by the Chinese veterans, the Chinese Benevolent Association in Vancouver and other supportive Canadians. During WWII, about 460 Canadian-born Chinese enlisted in the Canadian armed forces. This group of young and vibrant Canadian-born Chinese wanted to show loyalty to Canada, even though they were not recognized as citizens. They believed that through their good intentions and willingness to sacrifice themselves for the country, the Canadian Government and society at large would eventually recognize them and other Chinese settlers as Canadian citizens with the same rights and privileges as everyone else. After WWII these conscientious and dedicated Chinese veterans, with the support of other good-willed citizens, petitioned the Federal Government to have the Chinese Exclusion Act repealed and the head tax removed. They succeeded in their mission and helped Chinese immigrants regain their enfranchisement, and the Chinese settlers in Canada were given the opportunity to become Canadian citizens.

Later, this group of civic-minded Chinese Canadians pleaded for revision of the Immigration Act, so that Chinese Canadians would be able to sponsor their immediate family members to Canada for reunion. They succeeded, and the Family Reunion Immigration Policy became a reality. After the implementation of this policy, many Chinese Canadians sent for their spouses and children to join them in Canada.

In China, the people's desire to leave the country did not diminish. After the formation of the People's Republic in the early 1950s, Mao Zedong launched his land reform campaign. Private agricultural lands were confiscated, and the landlords were publicly denounced and humiliated. Many returning overseas Chinese were branded as capitalists and betrayers of the country, and they were often disgraced in public. Those people who had received remittances from overseas were reprimanded too.[6] Therefore, many people were living in fear and apprehension, and they were anxious to leave the country. However, it was not easy for anyone to leave China at that time because Mao's Government had restricted emigration. Many people, especially those in the Zhu Jiang Delta, escaped from their villages and took refuge in Hong Kong where they waited for opportunities to immigrate to Southeast Asia, Australia or North America.

In Canada, the immigration policy allowed Chinese Canadians to sponsor only their immediate family members to come over but no other relatives. Between 1950 and 1960 many Chinese immigrants came to Canada with 'bought papers', birth certificates belonging to the living or deceased children of old Chinese settlers who sold these papers to their desperate fellowmen in their villages or in Hong Kong, so that they could gain entry to Canada. Therefore, a fair number of Chinese immigrants, who entered into the country in that decade, carried a fictitious name, incorrect age and false marriage status. In 1960 the Diefenbaker Government introduced the Chinese Adjustment Program that offered amnesty to these illegal immigrants so that they could correct their status. This program was terminated in 1973.

In 1967, the Canadian Government introduced the point system in which the selection of immigrants was based on education, skills, and other factors that would contribute to the economic and cultural growth of this country. This immigration policy encouraged many Chinese professionals from Southeast Asia, Hong Kong and Taiwan to immigrate to Canada. At that time, unrest and racial discord were common in many Southeast Asia countries. For example, in 1965 bomb threats often occurred in Hong Kong, and in 1968 Malaysian Chinese were persecuted. Many Taiwan people who anticipated invasion from Mainland China made attempts to immigrate to North America. All these factors stimulated many Chinese from Southeast Asia to leave.

Many scholars and students from Southeast Asia dreamed of studying abroad, specializing in science and technology. Those families in Southeast Asia, who could afford it, usually sent their children to England, North America or Australia to continue their education. Some of these scholars and students came to Canada for further education. After they graduated from post secondary institutions, many applied for landed-immigrant status and remained in this country.

Meanwhile in the 1970s, the Canadian economy was booming and employment could be easily found. Big companies or corporations in Canada advertised job positions overseas to recruit skilled personnel to work in their mills or plants. Hence, Chinese engineers and tradesmen from Taiwan, Hong Kong, Malaysia, Singapore and Brunei applied for the positions and immigrated to Canada. As the Canadian economy became stronger, other professionals such as doctors, nurses, teachers and accountants also immigrated. In the last two decades, Canada increased trade with China, Japan, Hong Kong and Southeast Asia countries and encouraged business entrepreneurs and corporations from these countries to invest here. These trade initiatives, together with the uncertainty of Hong Kong's future after 1997, motivated many Chinese merchants and businessmen to immigrate with their families. Thus, the population of Chinese Canadians continues to grow.

The increase of Chinese immigration affected the population and occupations of Chinese Canadians in various communities in the Skeena-Bulkley Valleys, especially in Prince Rupert and Kitimat. During the last four decades, the Chinese Canadian population in Prince Rupert fluctuated between three to four hundred people. Instead of working mainly in fish canneries, these Chinese Canadians and immigrants worked in the Skeena Cellulose Pulp Mills as engineers and tradesmen. A few worked on the Canadian National Railway (CN) as yardmen, brakemen, mechanics and in other positions. In recent years more than ten restaurants that prepare authentic Chinese food have been established on Third Avenue in Prince Rupert.

Similarly, many Chinese Canadians and immigrants migrated in Kitimat, an industrial town whose growth was accelerated by the three industries, namely the Alcan Smelters, Eurocan Paper and Pulp, and the Methanx/Pacific Ammonia. In the early 1970s, when Alcan recruited skilled workers to work in its smelter, many Chinese Canadians and immigrants moved to Kitimat. Eurocan Paper and Pulp and Methanx/Pacific Ammonia also attracted a good number of skilled or professional people to the area. Many of them came from Southeast Asian countries such as Hong Kong, Taiwan, Singapore, Malaysia and Brunei. Their settlement stories in this relatively young community of Kitimat contrast vividly with those of the settlers who came to the Skeena-Bulkley Valleys at the turn of the nineteenth century.

A good number of early Chinese immigrants who went to the Skeena and Bulkley Valleys established their homes and raised their children in those areas. Some of their descendants are still living there. Prior to WWII, many of these Canadian-born Chinese were not given the opportunity to enter certain professions even though they had their education in the Canadian school system. After the Chinese Canadians regained their enfranchisement, these Canadian-born Chinese gradually integrated into the mainstream society. But they had to contend with the differences in cultures within the internal Chinese communities, especially when new Chinese immigrants drifted into the communities. Although all Chinese Canadians and immigrants came from the same roots, their cultures had evolved somewhat differently over the years, as they lived in different parts of the world and were affected by the environments in which they were brought up. In short, the Canadian-born Chinese also have their own versions of adjustments and cultural issues to tell about these settlements.

Clearly, the political, social and economic conditions of Canada and China as well as Southeast Asia have determined the patterns of Chinese immigration to Canada. Although early news reports, documents and books have recorded incidents and occurrences that fashioned the lives of the early Chinese immigrants, much is missing. Some writers have acknowledged the contributions made by the Chinese Canadians in this province, but they seldom mentioned the Chinese struggles and determination to make life possible in the face of prejudice and discrimination and their abilities to accept challenges in western society. Indeed, settlement stories are full of trial and error, success and failure, trust and suspicion, in the process of integration.

In some instances, the First Nation people showed acceptance and understanding of the Chinese immigrants. For example, many early Chinese immigrants were single men living alone without the warmth and love of their families. Some First Nation women showed compassion and affection to these lonely men and lived with them thus giving the men a sense of belonging. Unfortunately, their relationship often did not receive approval or recognition from either community. Many of these couples produced children who often experienced prejudice and discrimination in both communities and were often rejected because of their mixed blood. Their feelings of oppression and despair are rarely recorded.

As this book aims at recording human endeavors and personal achievements of the Chinese Canadians in the northwest of BC, extensive research has been carried out in the various archives of the Skeena-Bulkley region. Attempts were made to contact the Chinese communities to provide the history of the early settlements. Unfortunately, these communities are relatively small, and many old folk no longer live in the area. Their descendants and friends became the main source of information about the old-timers. These people also have many anecdotes regarding the Chinese Canadians living in smaller cities.

Many Chinese Canadians who migrated to these communities during the last decade do not have information about the early Chinese settlers, but they have their own settlement stories to tell. In communities where Chinese old-timers no longer live, and the current Chinese residents settled in the past ten years, other Canadians, those who are familiar with the life of the early Chinese, have supplied information. This book contains many interesting and colourful oral histories; the accuracy of these anecdotes, however, has been verified with other sources. If more than two persons relate similar incidents or stories, some truth can be assumed.

As Gordon Lam of Prince Rupert remarked, misunderstandings of one another's cultures and daily practices cause racial discord. Therefore, some Chinese cultural events and Chinese customs and practices are included as means of promoting awareness of Chinese culture. Indeed, the Chinese culture is deeply rooted in Chinese Canadians. Many Chinese Canadians and immigrants celebrate Chinese New Year, Dragon Boat Festival and Autumn Moon Festival with zeal, and observe Qing Ming, an important occasion for Chinese families to commemorate their ancestors. Nowadays, Chinese New Year has become such an important, interesting occasion that both Chinese and non-Chinese Canadians look forward to its colourful and joyous celebration. In addition, many Chinese Canadians have made great efforts to preserve their language by establishing Chinese schools. In this book readers can see how hard Chinese Canadians in smaller cities have worked to maintain their Chinese heritage.

I would like to point out that the Chinese language has a unified written system but many different spoken dialects. For example, the family name Chen (陈) in Mandarin or *Putonghua* may be pronounced as Chan or Chin in various Cantonese (广东) dialects. As Mandarin or *Putonghua* is the official Chinese language and is commonly used in Taiwan and Southeast Asia countries, *hanyu pinyin*, a phonetic system for Mandarin or *Putonghua* pronunciation, is included in a bracket behind certain terms as shown in the above sentence. However, names and terms familiar to local people are written as they are generally known.

Another aspect of the Chinese language, which creates confusion, is the order of Chinese names. Chinese people usually have three characters in their names. The first character is his or her family name. For example, Mah is the family name or the last name of the famous baker Mah Yoke Tong in

Smithers. He should be addressed as Mr. Mah and not Mr. Tong. Some of the Chinese Canadians and immigrants have acquired English names like Anita Tam. Specifically, Tam is her family name and Anita is the given name. Many old-timers usually registered their names with the prefix "Ah" to their family names such as Ah Lum or Ah Lock. This was done during registration when the early Chinese immigrants noticed that the immigration officers had difficulty in making out the spellings of the three characters in their names. Instead they just mentioned their family names with the prefix "Ah."

Quite often Canadians have misunderstood some of the Chinese names especially when their names contained a name similar to an English word. In the case of Joe Ham from Hazelton, people thought that his given name was Joe. In truth, Joe (周) is his family name in Taishan dialect meaning "Zhou" in *Putonghua* or "Chow" in Cantonese. This kind of confusion has not occurred in the last few decades as most of the recent immigrants understand the conventional Canadian naming system and register themselves accordingly. For example, Mung is the last name of Hing C. Mung, the President of the Alcan Asia Company. Terms that are known universally such as Mao Zedong, Beijing, Qing Ming festival and others are only written in *hanyu pinyin*.

In conclusion, a brief description of the location and a short account of the historical background of each town and city are included at the beginning of each chapter. This is to give readers some understanding of the environment where the Chinese Canadians have settled and the reasons why they chose to migrate to these areas. Also, the chapters are written in the order of chronological history when each town or city was first established, not according to their geographical location.

Chapter One

HAZELTON

The Jumping-off Point to the Omineca

Once upon a time, says a native legend, the entire nation of the Tsimpshian was dispersed after a massive flood. The Gitksan, an autonomous band of the Tsimpshian, eventually settled at the confluence of the Skeena and Bulkley Rivers. In 1860 when Thomas Hankin erected a trading post for the Hudson's Bay Company here, he named it Hazelton after the hazel bushes that grew profusely on the banks of the Skeena River.[1]

The rivers were teeming with fish during salmon runs, supplying food for the natives, who smoked and stored them for winter. The Rocher Deboule Mountains were a fur-trapping ground. The forests provided red cedar trees, used for constructing houses, totem poles, canoes, storage boxes and cedar bark clothing. This is a village where the Gitksan culture flourished. Even today their heritage can be seen in the K'san Village, a museum where native arts and crafts are housed, ancient artifacts displayed and totem poles planted majestically on the grounds. The Gitksan dances and songs are world famous. Nowadays, this place is commonly referred to as Hazelton or Old Hazelton to distinguish it from the nearby South Hazelton and New Hazelton.

Hazelton was one of the earliest villages in which whites and Chinese set up their homes in the Skeena-Bulkley Valleys. Europeans came to this area in 1866 during the construction of the Collins Overland Telegraph Line, which was to connect North America to Europe. Between 1870 and 1872 many gold miners, both white and Chinese, rushed to the Omineca gold fields. Those who came from the Cariboo usually traveled up the Fraser River to the Nechako then via the Stuart and Takla Lakes, or followed the telegraph trails to reach the mining areas in the Omineca. Others came up from the Pacific

Coast travelling on sternwheelers to Hazelton in order to reach their final destinations, thus making Hazelton the jumping-off point to the Omineca. These miners usually returned to Hazelton to spend their winters. The Gold Rush led to the arrival of pack-trains bringing provisions and mining supplies. It attracted journalists who reported on mining activities for their newspapers in Victoria, and it helped to establish mail services to the area. Merchants also came to Hazelton, to set up general stores, rooming houses, saloons and other businesses. Thus, settlements of different nationalities began to take place in Hazelton.

When the construction of the Grand Trunk Pacific Railway (GTP) reached the area around 1913, New Hazelton, a village about 10 kilometers southeast of Hazelton, was selected as the site of the GTP station. This event brought in thousands of construction workers, and almost robbed Hazelton of its role as a commercial center. However, Hazelton survived and retained its position as a navigation and commercial center until the railway became the main mode of transportation.

Hazelton circa 1872, one of BC's earliest busy city centres.
BC Provincial Archives

The Chinese Miners.

In the 1870 there were too many "humbugs" or false discoveries of gold in the north. Many white miners did not venture to the Omineca until Michael Burns and his party–who were sponsored by a group of Cariboo miners, businessmen and farmers to explore the area–confirmed that they had taken out $8,000 worth of gold from Vital Creek.[2] It was then that the Omineca Gold Rush began in earnest, and hundreds of miners reached Germansen Landing and Vital Creek in June 1871. When the news spread, Chinese miners wanted to migrate to the Omineca too. But they were prohibited to migrate to the area, just as they had been in the Cariboo. As they were afraid of bullies and assaults, they applied to the governor for protection and followed behind the white miners to the Omineca, anyway.

After arriving at Hazelton these miners, unlike the white miners who used horses or dog sleds, walked to their claims in the Omineca. Most of them were placer miners headed for Manson Creek, Tom Creek and Vital Creek. They carried their belongings and mining equipment on a pole about a metre and a half long, as they did in China. On one end of the pole they tied a sack containing simple provisions such as rice, tea, pickled vegetables, a pot, pan and a bag of clothing. On the other end they suspended a small folded tent and mining equipment such as a pan, shovel and spike. They balanced the pole, with its loads hanging at both ends, on their shoulders and carried their belongings to their mining claims. Once they reached their claims they quickly pitched their tents and lost no time digging and panning for gold.

Some of them would stay at their claims all year round. During the winter months, they dug tunnels and worked underground until they had enough gold or had finished working their claims before they came back to Hazelton. Those who returned for the winter carried their belongings in the same way they took them to their claims, but walked with snowshoes on the snow-covered ground. Initially it was quite a challenge for the Chinese miners to use snowshoes because they had never worn them in southern China. After learning how to use dog sleds and skis, they traveled in and out of their mining areas via these more conventional methods.

The size of the Chinese population in the Omineca is not easy to determine because the miners scattered themselves over Vital Creek, Germansen Creek, Tom Creek, Manson Creek and other small streams. Some of their names are listed in the gold commissioner's records, as they had to apply for mining licences to stake their claims. In 1874 it was estimated that one-third of the mining population in Omineca was Chinese; between 1901 and 1905 seventy-six Chinese miners were issued mining certificates in Manson Creek and Tom Creek.[3] On the list were some notable Chinese miners such as Ah Lock, Ah Lum and Ah Sam. Both Ah Lock and Ah Lum each had a stream named after them in the vicinity of Manson Creek. Ah Sam had a mining company that employed ten to twelve Chinese workers. Both Ah Lock and Ah Lum took native women as their wives. Ah Lock married Josephine Alexander, a Carrier, in the Babine area. Ah Lum married Esther Joseph, a Gitksan, in Hazelton, and the couple had four children, Peter, Tony, Thomas and Gwen. Their three sons were listed with the last name Ah Lum in the 1901 census on March 31. Gwen was born on November 1 of the same year.

Ah Lum was born in Guangdong, China, on October 13, 1843, and came to Canada in 1868. In the census he was listed as a Buddhist who spoke Chinese [presumably Cantonese]. On the Hudson's Bay Company records, Ah Lum is listed as having earned about $300 in six months. Perhaps Ah Lum, like other Chinese miners of his time, also trapped animals and sold the fur to the Hudson's Bay Company.

"We were told that grandpa Ah Lum had claims in Manson Creek area. But my mother and grandma always stayed in Hazelton. We assume that grandpa traveled back and forth between Manson Creek and Hazelton all the time," said Charlotte Sullivan, the granddaughter of Ah Lum. Sullivan is a Wing Chief of Gyedinguled, the Frog Land of the Gitksan.

Sullivan only knows bits and pieces about her grandfather from Gwen, her mother who, she said, had very fond memories of him, even though he did not spend much time with her when she was young. The Ah Lum family did not speak Chinese but Chinook. Neither did they observe any Chinese customs or festivals. Sullivan said her mother often talked about Ah Lum coming home with gold. Gwen remembered Ah Lum once giving her a good size gold nugget when he returned from the gold field. He made a piece of jewelry out of it and tied it to a silk handkerchief for his little daughter. Gwen loved the gift and always carried it with her.

"All the friends of Ah Lum said that he loved my mother the most. I suppose she was spoiled, being the youngest in the family," said Sullivan.

Unfortunately, Esther Joseph died when Gwen was only nine years old. After his wife passed away, Ah Lum wanted to take Gwen and the youngest brother back to China. The young boy did not want to go. Ah Lum, realizing that Gwen would be lonely and miserable without her brother in an unfamiliar country, decided against the plan. Finally he returned to China without his children, but maintained communication with them.

"Whenever my mother and uncles received a letter from their dad, they were excited and eager to know what he wrote. But they could not read

Chinese characters, so they usually took the letter to grandpa's Chinese friends in Hazelton or in Smithers who would translate the letter for them," said Sullivan. After Ah Lum went back to China, an aunt raised the children on the reserve.

"My mother did not have a very pleasant life in the native community," said Sullivan. "She was often looked down because she had mixed blood in her veins. Regardless, she was a very strong person and held her head up high. All of us children love and respect her. She has been a very good mom to us."

In later years, Peter, Tony and Thomas died of tuberculosis in Hazelton but Gwen lived until she was 93 years old. Sullivan has seen only a small but faded photograph of Ah Lum. She describes him as an old, round-faced man with a bald head but having a few strands of hair at the temples.

Like Ah Lum, many Chinese miners had their home base in Hazelton and spent their winters there. Unlike the Chinese miners in the Cariboo and the Fraser Valley, who segregated themselves from the whites and lived together in a Chinese settlement, the Hazelton Chinese pitched their tents or built their cabins wherever they found a space, and lived among the whites in the community. In spring they would return to their claims and continue mining. After they finished mining an area, they would stake or buy another claim from white miners who did not have the patience to pan for gold flakes or powder. These impatient white miners usually sold their claims to Chinese miners after the nuggets were gone.

Another well-known Chinese miner was Bang King, commonly known as "Irish" to his Canadian friends. In the late 1910s, he used to travel between Hazelton and Vital Creek. During summer he spent his time in Vital Creek mining; in winter he worked as a cook in the Hazelton Hospital.

"I do not know how he acquired the name 'Irish'," said Ward Marshall, who has lived in Hazelton since 1912. "I guess it was the attitude of white men at that time. They just attached an English name to the Chinese for easy pronunciation and remembering. But he was the biggest Chinese man I ever met. He was more than six feet tall with broad shoulders."

"He was quite an entrepreneur in Manson Creek," added Eric Janze who was born in Hazelton. "He did lots of gold mining in the Omineca and sent for his country men to work for him. He paid their head taxes to enter into this country."

"Irish had a nephew called Lee Yet Fey who worked in the hospital as a cook. When Lee left town Irish took his place in the hospital for some time," recalled Janze.

Irish's nephew, Lee Yet Fey, washing dishes
(circa 1939).

Photo courtesy Bill McRae

"In the thirties Irish went to Smithers and started a café. I used to play team sports and went on tournaments. Once, my team had a hockey match in Smithers. After the game we went to his café, and he fed us with roast beef, steaks, vegetable, beverages and desserts for 35 cents," recalled Marshall.

As the surrounding areas of Hazelton are rich in mineral deposits such as silver, copper, zinc, tungsten, molybdenum and other base metals; a number of mining companies operated in this area for many years. For example, the Silver Stand Mining Company produced silver and zinc; the Red Rose Mine extracted tungsten; and the Rocher Deboule Mine yielded copper, gold and silver. Many Chinese labourers had worked for these mining companies in the past. Dr. Eldon Lee treated a Chinese miner who was badly injured while working in one of these mines.

"I notice the Chinese people in Hazelton only came to the hospital when they were very ill or badly injured. But they donated generously to the hospital fund," said Dr. Lee.

Some senior Chinese were unwilling to go to hospital when they were sick. They believed that a hospital was a place for those who were on the verge of dying, and that ghosts were always hanging around hospitals ready to snatch their souls, thus hastening their deaths.

The Chinese Labourers in GTP and forestry industries.

By the time the construction of GTP reached New Hazelton in 1912, a number of Chinese cooks were employed in the construction camp. Ah Ding was one of the few Chinese labourers employed in the GTP section near New Hazelton. After a short while he was dismissed.

" I don't know why a Chinese man could not hold on to the job in the Government railroad," Marshall reminisced.

Maybe it was the clause "only white labourers," one of the agreements in the contract between the British Columbia Government and GTP.[4] For this reason, very few Chinese labourers were employed in the construction of the GTP. The Vancouver Trade and Labour Council also demanded that all employers were allowed only to employ Chinese labourers if they could not find a white labourer for the job. Perhaps Ah Ding lost his job after the Railroad Company found a white man to replace him.

Ah Ding lived in New Hazelton for some time and married a native woman from Hagwilget. The couple had a son whom they called Wily Ding who later changed his name to Will Sim and got a job on the GTP. He was an intelligent young man, and soon he was promoted to the position of a foreman. In Hazelton, he met and married a Gitksan woman. As she was an educated person she helped her husband with all the paperwork. Their children are still in Hazelton. One of Ah Ding's grandsons was the president of the ice arena project in Hazelton.

The construction of the GTP stimulated the establishment of a number of sawmills near Hazelton. Westar Timber Ltd. owned the largest sawmill in nearby Carnaby, which employed a large number of workers. This sawmill is still in operation. Other major forest industries included the Stege Logging Ltd. in New Hazelton, and Kitwanga Lumber Company in Kitwanga. A couple of smaller sawmills were located at Kispiox. Most of these sawmills were doing very well during World War II, as they supplied timber for the construction of army barracks in Terrace and Prince Rupert. In 1964 the establishment of the Skeena Cellulose Pulp Mill in Prince Rupert kept some of these sawmills going strong because wood chips were in great demand for the production of pulp. These forest industries employed a number of Chinese cooks in their camps.

The Chinese Businesses

By 1912, Hazelton was quite a busy and important place. It had a Government office, a police station and a jail, a newspaper office, two real estate offices and the Hudson's Bay Company with its liquor cellar. There were at least twelve different kinds of stores, including two famous business enterprises, the R.S. Sargent Ltd. and the Cunningham's Dry Goods. The Livery Stable, a mess house for young men, a water delivery business and a Chinese laundry are also listed in the 1912 land record of Hazelton.

Although gold mining gave the Chinese miners the possibility of getting rich, not all of them were that lucky. After they failed to realize their dreams of becoming wealthy some miners settled in Hazelton and took up any odd jobs or started businesses there. Three or four of the Chinese settlers worked as wood-choppers supplying fuel for the residents in Hazelton and vicinity. Most of the wood, delivered by horses and carts or sleds, came in two-metre lengths. The Chinese wood-choppers cut them into half-metre lengths for $3.50 per cord.

As the land office record indicates, there was a Chinese laundry in 1912. This Chinese laundry, known as Sun Lee Fat, was owned by Chow Tong. He operated the business in a log structure located near the bank of the Skeena River. In 1913, the land record also listed the place as Chow Tong Grocery Store, which provided laundry and bath services.

"He built a bathtub in a shed near his store," said Marshall. "He carried water from the Skeena River and boiled it in a large tin can on a brick stove. When a person wanted a warm bath, he would to go Sun Lee Fat with his own soap and towel. There he would pay Chow Tong 50 cents for a bath. Chow then would mix the hot water with some cold in a bathtub. You know, in those days people did not take a bath every day."

"In the early days there was no water supply or well in Hazelton," Marshall recalled. "A hotel dug a hole about 70 feet deep and could not get any water. Many people carried water from the Skeena River. They scooped up water from the Skeena at the dock near the Hudson Bay's Store. Some Chinese men carried water for the residents at 25 cents for a two-gallon can. The Chinese water carriers removed the lid from an empty two-gallon oil can and inserted a rectangular piece of small but sturdy wood to fit diagonally across the can. The piece of wood was then securely nailed to the rim. Taking two such cans, they filled them with water from the Skeena River. Attaching an iron hook at the center of the rectangular wood in each can, and tying the hook to one end of a rope and other end to a two-meter long wooden pole, they would balance the long pole, with a can of water hanging on each end, on their shoulders and carry the water to their customers. Ah Wing was one of the water carriers. He was a small man weighing about 75 kilograms. When he got older he used a cart to carry the buckets of water to his customers."

Two Chinese laundry businesses were in Hazelton about the same time as Sun Lee Fat. One-eye Wong owned one of the laundry businesses while Lee Chong operated the other. One-eye Wong was so called because he was blind in one eye. Arriving from Victoria where he had worked as a cook in a rich private home, he started work as a cook in a railroad camp. Afterwards, he started his laundry business in Hazelton. His little laundry shop was located near the bank of the Skeena River. Once a week he went to New Hazelton to pick up soiled linen from the railroad workers. He put it in two sacks and carried it home on his shoulder-pole. After the garments were washed and ironed, he delivered them to his customers the following week.

Lee Chong had his laundry in the same area. Unfortunately a big flood in June 1936 destroyed these two laundry shops; one of them was literally swept away by the roaring water of the Skeena, which was swollen from the melting snows from the mountains. After the flood, Lee Chong rebuilt his laundry store on higher ground. Wong did not do so but he remained in Hazelton and took whatever job was available until he passed away in 1943. He was buried in the cemetery of Hazelton. Lee continued his business until he died in 1969.

The 1936 Skeena flood was the worst one in the thirties. The swift, flowing water that surged over the riverbanks tore up bridges and railroad tracks. Thirty-three houses were washed away, and all buildings along the Main Street in Hazelton had to be evacuated. Canoes were used to transport people from the bank of the Skeena to higher ground. Water covered the village of Kitwanga, near Hazelton. The fast flowing water swept away a water tank and a pump house at a service station in Kitwanga. Communication was cut off for more than three days.[5] After the flood, some good citizens went up to the Chinese laundry men to express their regrets and sympathy. One of the Chinese men responded, "Well, if anyone of you have clothing with me, you have to collect them at the mouth of the Skeena."

"It is admirable to find them retaining their sense of humor after their loss," commended Jessi Gould, a senior citizen in Hazelton.

The Chinese Restaurants

Besides owning laundries, the early Chinese immigrants operated grocery stores and Chinese restaurants too, the latter of which are fondly remembered for the delicious Chinese food that they served. In Hazelton names of Chinese restaurants such as the Royal Café, Rex Café, Joe Ham Café, BC Café and OK Café are found in the land office records and in the early donation lists of the Hazelton Hospital. On January 30, 1921, a fire destroyed the Royal Café, the

BC Café and the Omineca Hotel. Sam Lee, one of the four owners of the Royal Café, was burned to death. When the fire broke out, all four of them were asleep in the building; all escaped except for Lee. His partially-charred body was found on the remains of the mattress in his bedroom. The fire was caused by an over-heated stovepipe containing accumulated creosote.[6] In the early days, very few buildings had brick chimneys, and most people burnt wood to warm their houses as there was no electricity or natural gas. Unfortunately wood, especially green or unseasoned, produces creosote which catches fire easily. After the fire, the BC Café was rebuilt but not the Royal Café.

When the BC Café was rebuilt, six bedrooms were added to the top floor. These bedrooms were used to provide accommodation for Chinese visitors and seasonal workers. The ground floor remained as a Chinese restaurant. Like other restaurants in Hazelton, the BC Café has changed hands many times in its history. Once, Joe Ham, Sing Lee and four other partners operated the restaurant. Joe was a very good cook and many people, including tourists from the States, loved to eat in his restaurant. He was also an excellent story-teller and willing to share his stories with anyone who cared to listen. His good friends in the Bulkley Valley included Eric Janze, Chuck Morris and Johnny Dunlop.

Chinese immigrants in Canada followed the traditional Chinese way of life very strictly in the early 1900s, and the next story reveals just how different things were then. It involves Joe Ham's friend Eric Janze.

Janze had two daughters by his first marriage. A few years after his first wife passed away, Janze remarried and his new wife gave birth to a son. All the Chinese men in Hazelton were very happy for him. To Joe Ham, it was a joyful and important occasion for a celebration; he held a big party for the Janze family and invited all his good friends–whites, Chinese and natives–to join him and the Janzes for the celebration. At the party, Joe Ham toasted Eric Janze and said, "Now everything is all right [with you] because you have a son."

This short speech reveals the importance of a male member in Chinese families, especially in traditional ones. Even today, many Chinese families still prefer a son to a daughter because a son will carry and perpetuate the family name. In traditional Chinese homes, sons are expected to look after the aged parents and the welfare of the family. They are the ones to inherit the estate of the father, if there is any. Daughters do not inherit anything.

When Joe Ham reached retirement age, he wanted to go back to China to spend his sunset years there, but wanted to get his old age pension before he left. In order to get the pension, he had to become a Canadian citizen. He asked Chuck Morris and Johnny Dunlop to stand as witnesses for him in court. When the day arrived for him to get his citizenship, both Morris and Dunlop went with him to Prince Rupert. After Joe took his oath, Judge Harvey asked him a number of questions. Some questions should have been answered with a "yes" but he replied "no" or vice versa. For example, Judge Harvey asked him, "Do you want to go back to China?"

He replied, "No".

Then he was asked, "Are you a communist?"

He gave "yes" for an answer. After some questioning, Judge Harvey called the two witnesses to come forward to ask them about Joe Ham. Both Morris and Dunlop testified that Joe was a very good citizen. They told Judge Harvey that Joe gave the incorrect answers because he was nervous. Upon their recommendation, Joe was granted Canadian citizenship. A few months later he went back to China with Sing Lee, one of his business partners.

"To recall that day when Joe Ham was in court to get his citizenship, I still find it rather amusing. But we felt quite nervous for him, too, when he gave the wrong answers," commented Morris.

In the sixties, Jackson Eng Wah Hong and his wife took over the restaurant and operated it until they retired in 1984. Greg and Anna Chan then took over the ownership and have operated the restaurant ever since. Before the Chans came to Hazelton, they worked in Smithers with Jim Woo, their brother-in-law, at the Northern Star Café, and later with Michael Jang at the Tyee Restaurant, also in Smithers.

Like many new immigrants, the Chans went through a period of adjustment after arriving in this country on November 27, 1979. They came from the Xinhui county in Guangdong and immigrated to Canada under the sponsorship of Jim Woo.

"When we first arrived we found life rather isolated," said Anna Chan, "Although we were staying with the family of my brother-in-law, we still felt lonely. They were restaurant people who were not at home most of the time. Their children went to school and had their own activities. All of them were very busy people."

" We found the language barrier the greatest challenge," Greg Chan commented. "As we could not speak English to talk with our neighbors, our communications were limited to members of the Woo family."

" A few years ago I met a friend in Vancouver who immigrated from China not too long ago," Greg continued. "He could not find any job in the Lower mainland because he could not speak English. I invited him to come and work for me in the café. He worked for us only about three months and left.

He found life isolating and boring here. In this small village all the shops are closed after 5 pm, whereas in Hong Kong and Canton (Guangzhou) life begins at eight or nine in the evening. Illuminated by colorful neon signs, supermarkets, shops, restaurants, and other stores remain open until midnight in many Chinese cities. Entertainment is plentiful. The winter here is too long. Although we have winter in Guangdong, it was never as cold as here, nor was there snow."

Indeed, life in a foreign country has always been challenging for new immigrants, whether they are rich or poor, young or old, coloured or white. New immigrants not only have to cope with language and cultural differences but also with some of the physical and social elements such as the weather, transportation, neighborhood, and medical facilities, especially in northern communities. One consolation to the Chans is that the people in Smithers and Hazelton have been warm and friendly to them.

Before they immigrated to Canada, Anna was a doctor in Zhongshan Medical College in Guangdong and had been practicing medicine since 1965. Her husband Greg was a tradesman. Both of them were unable to pursue their professions because they were handicapped by their lack of English. Anna felt that at the age of forty, it would not be easy for her to pick up the English necessary to go back to medical school. Financially, she simply could not afford to go back to school. Her father and mother in-law, who were in Vancouver, needed help and support. Therefore, she decided to spend her time raising the children and helping her husband to manage the restaurant.

The OK Café was another popular restaurant in the early days. It was owned and operated by the father of Lee Chong, the laundry man. After the disastrous flood in 1936, Lee's father left Hazelton and started another restaurant business in Vanderhoof. Lee Chong took over his father's restaurant business and called it the Shanghai Café. He and his girl friend, Mary Ann, lived on the upper floor of the cafe. Mary Ann was known as "Wild Cat" in Hazelton. One morning, a neighbour witnessed Mary Ann chasing Chong on the roof. She held a broom in her hand and swung it at Chong so hard that she had to hold on to the roof to keep herself from falling. It is not known if she was a native or white, but she was definitely not Chinese because Chinese women did not arrive at Hazelton until 1950.

The Shanghai Café has changed hands a number of times. In the early fifties, Jim Lee bought the restaurant and operated it for about ten years. Jim Lee was nicknamed "Speed" in Hazelton because he could not walk fast. People were always urging him to speed up, and so he was stuck with the nickname.

"But I tell you, Speed is a wonderful person," said Morris, a retired salesman in Smithers, who delivered meat to most of the Chinese restaurants from Kitimat to Vanderhoof for more than twenty years.

"He is my good friend," continued Morris. "After he moved to Prince Rupert, he sent me an envelope filled with old money bills without a note or any explanation, but I knew it was from him."

After Jim Lee left for Prince Rupert, Wing Eng became the owner of the Shanghai Café and operated it for some time before Charlie Chow and Gim Wong took over the business in the early sixties. In 1963, Wong sold his share to Chow, who changed its name to Sunrise Café. Chow operated it until he returned to Prince George in the early eighties. Today a Vietnamese owner runs the Sunrise Café.

Bob Mah, the Chinese alderman.

Bob Mah, also known as Bob Eng, was an outstanding Chinese Canadian in Hazelton. Many senior folks acknowledge his volunteer services and contributions to the community. In the beginning Mah operated a bakery in town that sold bread, pies, apple turnovers and cookies. He also delivered his goods to the mining camps in the surrounding areas. Later, he opened a supermarket and a wholesale business to supply goods to stores in the surrounding areas. While living in Hazelton, two more children were added to the family.

In his leisure, he devoted his time to community work. He was elected as an alderman and spearheaded the Hazelton ice arena project. He spent much time and effort to ensure the completion of the project. He integrated well into the Canadian society and was appreciated by all his friends and many others in Hazelton.

"Bob practiced many Canadian customs," said Marshall. "I remember for a couple of Christmas Eves, he dressed up as Santa Claus, piled bags of gifts on a dog sled and went from house to house to deliver Christmas gifts. He gave people oranges, apples, candies or anything he could think of as Christmas presents."

Although Bob Mah had adopted a liberal attitude, he still held on to the belief that a Chinese girl should only go out with a Chinese boy. This belief puzzled many of his Canadian friends.

"April, Bob's youngest daughter, was quite a pretty girl," commented Marshall, "She went to high school with my boy. One year, they had a school dance. My boy asked her if she could go to the dance with him. She told him to ask her dad. When my boy approached Bob, he would not give consent. The young people were upset. After a few days when the dust settled down, Bob sent a young Chinese man to give us the reasons. Maybe the messenger did not do a good job in explaining because I still find it rather illogical."

Indeed, it is difficult for others to understand the Chinese beliefs and values. Even today, many Chinese people still expect or prefer their children go out with Chinese Canadians, who are not only compatible in financial status and family background but also in achievement and appearance. It takes time for the traditional Chinese Canadians to change their preferences and to give up their practices, especially for those who live in a large Chinese community where peer pressure is present. It also takes time for them, including new immigrants, to understand and accept the practices and customs of other Canadians. By the same token, other Canadians often have difficulties in understanding the Chinese beliefs and values which appear contrary to Canadian expectations.

Despite Mah's attempt to hold on to his Chinese beliefs, two of his children married white people. His oldest son met an Italian girl in high school and married her after they graduated from high school. Then they left Hazelton and moved to Vernon. April married a Chinese man, but their marriage did not work out. She divorced her husband and left town. In Vancouver she met an American, married him, and now lives in the State of Washington. In 1958, Mah, his wife Helen and two children, moved to Hazelton from Prince George. After 1985 when Mah was diagnosed with stomach cancer, the family left Hazelton for the lower mainland. In 1987 Bob Mah died and was buried in Vancouver. Two years later Helen also passed away from cancer.

The Chinese Festivals and Recreation.

Bob Mah attempted to keep some of the Chinese traditions alive. During Qing Ming he would gather a group of Chinese people to go to the cemetery to pay respect to those who were buried there. They brought with them rice wine, steamed rice, fowls, fruits, candles and incense, and paper money. Many Canadian children would go along to watch the Chinese rituals. Mah would give 25 cents to each child who accompanied his group.

"The Chinese people would pour the rice wine on the ground as a gesture to offer drinks to the deceased," said Marshall. "They would scatter some steamed rice as a token of sharing food with the spirits. Bob called it 'the devil chasing festival'."

Actually, Qing Ming is known as the festival of light and brightness. It usually takes place around Easter and lasts for a month. The Chinese go to the graveyard, usually on the first day of the festival, to clean up the tombs of their ancestors and pay respect to the deceased. Since the great majority of the early Chinese immigrants came here as single men, they did not have their immediate families in this country to carry out the observance. Many of them, including those who died in mines and in railroad constructions, were buried in this country. Others, who could not afford to return home, also were buried here.

Although some of the people going to the cemetery during Qing Ming may not have met the deceased, they looked upon them as friends or relatives, especially those who came from the same village. Chinese people believe that when a person dies, his spirit remains. These lonely spirits could only rest in peace after their bones were taken and buried in their home villages. As long as their skeletons remained buried in this land, their spirits had to be appeased. During Qing Ming and Cong Yang festivals, the traditional Chinese Canadians go to the cemetery to pay respect to those who are buried there.

After Bob Mah left Hazelton, some of Chinese Canadians in Hazelton and the surrounding areas continued with the tradition.

"There are only about three Chinese graves in the Hazelton cemetery," said Tim Leong, the owner of the Totem Café. "We have been going to the cemetery for the past twenty years during Qing Ming. Now there are not many Chinese Canadians in this area. Somehow, the four or five Chinese Canadians families in this area just stopped going in the last two years."

"In the early days when a Chinese died he was buried here," said Ward Marshall, an undertaker in Hazelton in earlier years. "After awhile their bones were exhumed, washed and cleaned, and put back in a jar which was re-buried in the same spot. Later, the jar was dug up and sent to Victoria, where it was dispatched together with others to China. This is why there are so few Chinese graves in the cemetery now."

Bone exhumation has been carried on in China for many years. The fact that the early Chinese immigrants wanted their bones to be sent back to China reflects their attitude toward foreign lands. Their main purpose of coming to the gold mountains was to find their fortune so that they could improve the lives of their families. They dreamed of going home to spend their sunset years with their loved ones. Unfortunately, many of them died with their dreams unfulfilled. So, in the early days their friends and relatives, together with the Chinese Benevolent Association in Victoria, helped ship the bones back to their villages in China. For hygienic reasons the Canadian Government prohibited exhumation after World War II. Today some of the remote villages in China still carry out bone exhumation as a means to increase land for cultivation. Some old-timers believe that exhumation symbolizes a form of resurrection because during exhumation the remains are once again exposed to light.

The Chinese residents in Hazelton often gather together to celebrate Chinese New Year. They do not have a big communal celebration like those in bigger cities because the Chinese community consists of only five or six Chinese families, including a couple of overseas Chinese families from Vietnam.

"We just do not have the time and resources to host a large celebration in the community," said Tim Leong. "It is quite expensive to transport some of the delicacies and traditional Chinese New Year food from Vancouver. Instead, the few Chinese families gather to have a good meal in one of our restaurants to replace the traditional Chinese reunion dinner at home."

In early times, the explosion of firecrackers during the spring festival would signal that Chinese New Year had arrived. Although the early Chinese residents might not know the exact date of the Chinese New Year they would know the occasion had arrived from the letters they received from home or from merchants in the lower mainland. As the Chinese New Year lasts for fifteen days, they could celebrate the event any time during this period. During the celebration the Chinese merchants would give their Canadian friends lily bulbs, leechee nuts and Chinese candies.

"Joe Ham used to invite his Canadian friends to a big meal to celebrate Chinese New Year," said Chuck Morris. "My family always got invited to the big treats."

There is no evidence that the Chinese settlers in Hazelton celebrated other important Chinese festivals such as the Dragon Boat Festival and Autumn Moon Festival. It was difficult for the early Chinese to remember the dates because they had no Chinese calendar. Even today the Chinese Canadians do not make a big fuss over these festivals. They talk about the festival, and order special food such as *zongzi*, steamed gelatin rice wrapped in bamboo leaves, for the Dragon Boat Festival, and moon cakes for the Autumn Moon Festival from Vancouver or Edmonton.

Chinese Canadians, past and present, celebrate Christmas with as much zeal as other Canadians. In Hazelton, they spend time decorating their shops and homes, exchanging gifts and enjoying a holiday break, giving them a couple of days to relax and to have some fun. Playing mahjong is the favourite pastime of many Chinese Canadians and has become a part of their holiday celebrations.

The BC Café in 1997 - a popular Chinese restaurant in Hazelton since 1950.

Photo by Lily Chow

In the 1950s five partners were operating the BC Café. In the restaurant there were two doors leading off from the dining room; one led directly to the kitchen and the other to a small room where the partners played mahjong. When business was slow, four out of the five partners would go to back and play mahjong, leaving one managing the café. When business picked up during lunch or dinnertime, they just covered the mahjong tiles with newspaper and went back to work. Afterward they would continue with the game. According to Ward Marshall, when the Chinese restaurant closed down during Christmas holidays, the sound produced by the slapping of the mahjong tiles on the table could be heard almost all day long.

In the late 1950s a few Chinese families gradually arrived and settled in Hazelton. The Chinese children joined other Canadians in outdoor activities such as skating and skiing during the Christmas season. The Chan family aside, almost no Chinese resident went to church during Christmas season.

Although the Chinese residents enjoyed gambling, no evidence of an organized gambling den has been found in town. Nor did any Chinese organization exist there. The archives of the Chinese Freemason Society headquarters in Vancouver contain no mention of a lodge in Hazelton. The absence of any Chinese organization in Hazelton is surprising to historians and others who know the role of Chinese societies. In other mining areas, such as in the Cariboo and the Fraser Valley, Chinese societies helped and supported Chinese immigrants by finding them jobs and looking after their welfare. The Chinese population in Hazelton was largely made up of placer miners, who did not require agents to find them jobs, and small business owners, who were more or less self-employed. The miners moved around all the time and only congregated in Hazelton during winter. As indicated, the community in general was friendly and kind; it was unnecessary for the Chinese residents to form an organization to protect themselves.

The Spirit of the Chinese Community.

The early Chinese immigrants went to Hazelton intending to go to the Omineca gold fields to find the yellow treasure. Therefore, they stopped at Hazelton only briefly before proceeding further inland. After the Omineca Gold Rush (1871-1875) Chinese immigrants had increasing difficulty in finding work in mainstream industries and businesses. Anti-Chinese movements began to surface, especially in the lower mainland. Some of the placer miners then settled in Hazelton to start small businesses. Their ventures not only helped them to make a living but also provided jobs for their fellow countrymen. Although the Chinese population in Hazelton has been small and fluctuated throughout history, many Chinese immigrants have left fond memories behind as they attempted to contribute to the development and growth of the community.

"In the early days, the Chinese immigrants did not have their families or children with them, but they still helped the school's fund-raising events and often attended meetings of the Parent/Teacher Association," said Eric Janze. Numerous Chinese names and businesses such as, Joe Ham, Lee Chong, Jim Lee, Wing the water carrier, OK Café, BC Café and others were listed as donors in the Hazelton Hospital Annual Reports between 1921 and 1938.

"Although there were only about 30 Chinese people living in Hazelton between 1957 and 1959, many of them donated money generously towards the hospital funds," said Dr. Eldon Lee, a non-Chinese doctor operating in Hazelton at the time.

Indeed, the Chinese residents have been kind and helpful to their neighbors in the village and they continue to be so, doing whatever they can for the community. Bob Mah was a fine example of a Chinese Canadian who volunteered his service to the community and attempted to reach out to others. The restaurant owners were noted for their generosity in giving credit to their clients during difficult times.

It is encouraging to note that few records of prejudice and discrimination against the Chinese immigrants were found other than the systemic discrimination imposed by the BC and Federal Governments. Some disputes over land claims in some mining areas were noted, but such incidents were common among all miners during all the Gold Rush periods. Unfortunately, Hazelton lost its role of a navigation center after the completion of the GTP in 1916. Its position of a road transportation hub connecting the various towns in the Bulkley Valley was reduced after the completion of Highway 16 which bypasses Hazelton. These factors have reduced Hazelton to a quiet place. Although the heyday of Hazelton is over, it still retains its unique characteristic of a historic village rich in native culture, taking visitors back to the past and offering them a sense of simplicity and tranquillity.

Chapter Two

PORT ESSINGTON

The Coastal Region in the North

The north coast of British Columbia consists of many inlets, bays, rivers and streams. Two large rivers, the Skeena and the Nass, drain their waters into the Pacific Ocean and are of great economic importance to the northwest region of this province. These two rivers function as migratory routes for the Pacific salmon returning to their spawning grounds. The deep sea off the coastline is dotted with numerous islands, such as the Smith, Watson, Kaien, Ridley and other islands that create many inner passages for boats and canoes to enter into Port Essington, Port Edward and Prince Rupert. These inner passages also offer ways by which Pacific salmon enter into the two main rivers.

In the good old days, millions of fish were visible near the surface of the water, especially at the mouths of the Skeena and Nass Rivers and in the inner passages. This abundant food source encouraged commercial fishing and the establishment of fish canneries in the north coast. The first fish cannery, the Inverness Cannery, was established on the north bank of the Skeena River at its entrance in 1876. By the 1900s Port Essington had eight fish canneries, and Port Edward and its vicinity had five. As years went by, other fish canneries also established on Kaien Island, at the mouth of the Nass River and at nearby bays. Places like Port Essington and Port Edward, where five or more canneries had been established, gradually developed into small villages.

A Fishing Village of the Past

Port Essington was located on a rugged peninsula west of Ecstall River, about thirty kilometers away from the mouth of the Skeena River. In 1870, Robert Cunningham and his family settled here and established two sawmills

Port Essington circa the 1900's. This once booming fishing town is now but a distant memory, becoming nothing more than charred remains in the (final) fire of 1965.

BC Provincial Archives

and a general store. When prospectors and miners from the Pacific coast went to the interior via the Skeena River, they usually stopped at Port Essington to get their provisions and mining equipment. At that time there was no road or railway, and the Skeena River was the only way by which the gold seekers could travel to the Omineca. Later it became a route to the Klondike. In 1883, Cunningham set up his first fish cannery in Port Essington. Soon other merchants established fish canneries in this village.

When the Grand Trunk Pacific Railway Company (GTP) proposed to build its line from the Kaien Island to join the railway extension from Alberta, people expected that the railway would pass through Port Essington. The railway was built on the north bank of the Skeena River across from Port Essington, located on the south bank. The many surveyors, railway contractors and labourers camped across from Port Essington during the construction of the railway. These people often sailed across the Skeena to Port Essington to shop or spend their weekends. All these events stimulated the growth and development of this fishing village.

The centre of Port Essington consisted of narrow streets with wooden boardwalks, and thirty or more buildings including two churches, two schools and a community hall. During its heyday Port Essington had a bank, two hotels with bars and saloons, restaurants, butcher shops, general stores, a drug store, a dress shop and a laundry. In the community there were three newspapers, *The Port Essington Loyalist*, *The Port Essington Star* and *The Port Essington Sun*. In addition, an employment agency and a medical clinic, with dentist and doctor, were located there. The chief industries were sawmills and fish canneries. Once this village boasted a population of approximately 3000 people in the summer but only about 500 after the fishing season.

The Fish Canneries

Port Essington has very little flat land, and mountain cliffs drop almost perpendicular to the narrow beach. Hence, all the fish canneries were located along the narrow beach with their buildings and wharves erected on large poles driven into the sea floor. Each cannery had its own can-making section, butchering house, filling department, soldering area, fish cooking or steaming structures and a storage warehouse. A boat service building, net making and repair shop, blacksmith and machine shops were included in most canneries.[1] Every cannery contained at least one mess hall or a cafeteria with kitchen facilities to serve meals to the workers. Usually Chinese cooks were employed to prepare the food.

All of the canneries followed a similar pattern in their management and employed four ethnic groups, namely European, First Nations, Japanese and Chinese, in their operations. The Europeans or whites were the administrators, clerks, mechanics, engineers and fishermen. The native men went out with the white people to fish in the rivers or in the open sea. The native women made and mended nets for their husbands and other fishermen. When fish canning began, many of these women were hired to work with the Chinese workers in the canneries. The Japanese worked as carpenters and wood-cutters. During early winter these Japanese went to the bush to cut wood and turned the wood into charcoal for the canneries. In spring they cleaned and repaired boats and carried out maintenance work on the wharves as well as in the canneries. The Chinese workers were the main labour-force in many canneries although none of them went out to the sea as commercial fishermen.

The Roles of the Chinese Workers

Usually the Chinese seasonal workers arrived just before the salmon run. The first task they had to do was to make cans. They cut out strips of tin metal, rolled them on a cylindrical mold and soldered the sides together to form a round cylinder. They also punched off round discs from the metal sheets to fit the opening ends of the cylinder. Then they soldered a disc to one end of the hollow cylinder to form an open can. The work was done all by hand, requiring speed and precision in cutting the tin strips. In the early days a charcoal burner was used to heat up the soldering equipment and to melt lead for sealing up the can. Thus, can-makers were exposed to fumes from the charcoal burners as well as from the liquid lead. Around 1915, a sanitary can-making machine was introduced to the canneries to replace manual can-making.

When the fish arrived, they were thrown into a sluice box that transferred them to a scow. One or two Chinese workers, clad in heavy water-proof capes, hats and pairs of long oilskin boots, would sort out the fish with a metal fork and toss them into boxes. Although fishing nets were made in such a way that only one kind of fish could be caught in a net there were always sockeyes, cohoe, chum, pink salmon and other fish mixed up in one catch. These fish sorters had to be able to recognize the different fish and separate them into appropriate boxes. They had to work fast, for they were paid according to how many boxes of fish they could sort out in a day. The fish sorting job not only required muscular strength but also the ability to maintain balance in the sorting process while standing on a wet and slimy surface. On at least one occasion, a Chinese sorter was covered in fish up to his neck when he slipped and fell near the end of a sluice causing a load of fish to skid down upon him[2]. After sorting, workers carried the boxes of fish to the canning plant. In later years the fish were delivered to the canning plants via an escalator.

In the canning plant, a group of Chinese workers butchered the fish on a long bench while they stood on one side. These workers, holding a razor sharp knife, cut off the heads and fins, slit open the belly of each fish, removed its guts and sliced the fish into halves lengthwise. Some of these Chinese "slitters" could butcher 2000 fish in a 10-hour day[3]. This task required good hand-eye coordination to avoid injury from the sharp knives. In addition, the slitters were expected to work fast. The butchered fish were then pushed to the opposite side of the bench where native women would scrub off the scales, carry out the final trimming, and wash the fish with water from hoses hanging above the bench or wash them in a water tank at the end of the butchering table.

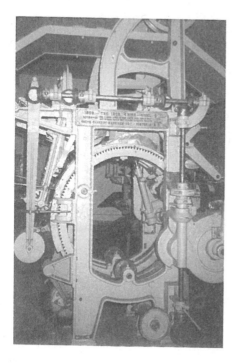

The 'Iron Chink', on display at the North Pacific Cannery.

Photo by Lily Chow

In 1905, a butchering machine, the "Iron Chink," was introduced to all the fish canneries in an attempt to replace the Chinese workers. The management claimed that this apparatus could perform as fast as the Chinese butchers could, if not faster. At that time the anti-Chinese movement was simmering and the Chinese immigrants were labeled with many derogatory names such as "Chinamen," "Celestials," "Chinks" and others. The name, "Iron Chink," therefore, reflects the discriminatory attitude of the management. The Iron Chink could not replace the Chinese workers though it did help to speed up the slaughtering process; the more fish cut, the more Chinese workers needed in the canning process.

After the fish were cut, the remnants such as guts, fins and scales were scrapped and dropped to the shore through a large hole in the bench. There they would be washed away by the rising tides. The sea gulls would consume the discarded offal floating on the water. Today, these remnants are collected to produce fertilizer.

Before the introduction of the Iron Chink, the clean fish would be delivered to another group of Chinese workers who cut them into uniform pieces. Later on, the cutter's job was replaced by a Gang Knife, a machine consisting of a series of parallel sharp blades that cut the fish into appropriate lengths to fit the various sizes of cans. The native women then filled the cans with these pieces and put the open cans on a tray. Other Chinese workers would cap and seal the cans and take them to a steam box to cook for 30 minutes.

After the cooking, the Chinese workers pulled out each tray containing the hot cans and punched a tiny hole in each can to release the steam. Immediately, they sealed the hole with a drop of melted copper. Then another group of Chinese workers stacked the sealed cans on trays and pushed them into a retort, or boiler, to cook for another 50 minutes. Afterward, each can was dipped into lye water to remove grease and put on the floor to cool. In this section the Chinese workers were exposed to intense heat from the steam boxes and retorts and had to be able to tolerate the high temperature from the hot cans when they were dipped into lye water. They also had to put up with the harmful side effects of lye, molten metal and the horrible smell.

Finally, the Chinese workers would brush a layer of lacquer on each can to prevent rusting and paste labels on the cans by hand before the workers packed the cans into boxes for shipment. In the early days the boxes were not made of cardboard, but strips of wood. Chinese workers were also hired to make these boxes.

Accommodations

All canneries provided living quarters for their staff and workers, but each ethnic group was segregated from one another. Some experts assert that the separate housing was for cultural and linguistic reasons, believing each group would feel more comfortable living with its own people. Others maintain that it was a management strategy to deal with employees. David Boyce, a writer and a guide in the North Pacific Cannery Village Museum, remarked that if the different racial groups did not have the opportunity to interact with each other socially, then each group would not know about the wages of the other national groups. The living quarters for the First Nation people and the Chinese workers were found at the rear of the canning plants. The housing for the First Nation people consisted of rows of cabins whereas the Chinese workers lived in bunkhouses. Both First Nations people and Chinese workers were hired on a seasonal basis.

The Chinese bunkhouses

These were barn-like wooden buildings with two storeys that housed between 50 to 60 people in each. The downstairs usually consisted of a few rooms with bunk beds, and a long hall furnished with rough wooden tables, stools, two or three cupboards for dishes, and a wood stove. The Chinese workers were not expected to cook in the bunkhouse, as they would be too busy working in the canneries. The mess hall supplied them with their daily meals. When they became tired of the mass-produced meal, they usually boiled water to make themselves a cup of tea or cooked some rice over the wood stove in the evening. Their home-made meals were simple usually consisting of rice, salt fish, pickled vegetables or fermented bean curds. After finishing their meal, the workers would play games and socialize around the wood stove.

The upstairs of the building contained rows of bunk beds. When the workers arrived at the canneries, they carried with them pillows, bamboo mats to put on the bed, mosquito nets and thin blankets. They worked from late spring to the fall when the weather was warm and the surrounding area was swarming with mosquitoes. In some bunkhouses there was a verandah for them to sit around and smoke their pipes in the evening.

The Chinese workers always found a spot close to their bunkhouse to plant vegetables so that they would have a fresh supply of produce while they were working in the canneries. Usually, they would fence up a section where they kept fowls and pigs. These animals, especially the pigs, were fed with slops or leftovers from the mess hall.

Behind the bunkhouse they enclosed an area for showers. Near the enclosure, they built a hot water tank heated by wood in a clay stove. It was not easy to find fresh water in Port Essington, so the workers would take turns to go to the nearby spring to get water. Some water was heated, the rest left cold for showers and other uses. When they washed themselves, they took their own basin, a container to scoop both the hot and cold water, mixed them until the temperature of the water was right before they scrubbed themselves.

China Bosses

The contractors or 'China Bosses' were employees or partners of some well-known employment agencies such as Chock On, Lew Bing, Yip Sang and other companies in Vancouver. In the early days each cannery had at least one China Boss, or contractor who was knowledgeable about the canning procedures. In Port Essington, Fan You was the China Boss in the Cunningham Cannery, Mah Toy in the British American and Lee Lim in the Skeena Commercial. In early May, these contractors brought the Chinese workers to the various canneries, as they were required to make cans before canning commenced. After the workers arrived at the cannery, the contractors assigned the various tasks and then supervised them. In most canneries, it was the China Bosses who also contracted and paid native women to clean fish and stuff the pieces into cans. The whole contract system relieved the cannery manager of personnel problems and placed the recruitment of labourers and the financial risk on the contractors.[4]

However, no record of contractors suffering financial loss has been found because the contract system was set up in such way that the Chinese workers would absorb any loss incurred, especially in poor seasons. The contractors were given a certain sum of money to transport the crew from Vancouver; the number of workers they transported determined the amount of money they received. This money was to spend on passages, food and any overhead costs but not wages..

The workers were paid at the end of the fishing season on a piecework basis, meaning how many cans did they make, the number of fish they slaughtered and other types of piecework they performed in the season. In a good year they would be able to earn more because there were more fish for them to butcher and can, while in a poor season they would take less money home. Therefore, there was no way in which the contractors could lose money.

Most contractors also operated businesses in the community. On the way to the canneries, the contractors carried with them some Chinese delicacies, tobacco leaves, rice wine, workmen's clothing, wooden clogs, flannel slippers; and personal articles such as tooth brushes, razors and such to sell to the Chinese workers. These items came from merchants in Vancouver or were imported directly from Hong Kong & Guangzhou. The Chinese workers would purchase these goods from the contractors. Of course, they had to pay more for them, since the village shops probably did not carry them. In this way the contractors made substantial profits from the merchandise they sold.

The contractors kept close contact with the employment agencies in Vancouver and sent them reports regularly during the canning season. The Chock On Fond records kept in UBC Special Collections, contain numerous reports and correspondence, written in Chinese, about the production of canned fish, the well-being of the workers and the working conditions in the canneries. One letter mentioned that the Chinese bunkhouse in one of the canneries was very large and contained bunk beds, two large tables and a good number of stools and benches, and two cooking stoves, but no place to put their garbage. Another letter informed Chock On Agency that very little flat land was available to cultivate a vegetable garden at a certain cannery, and the crew requested Chock On to send up produce and other food items.

Some contractors complained that certain newcomers were unfamiliar with the tasks; consequently, the production of that season was less than expected. Other contractors asked Chock On Agency to stop shipping groceries and other perishable goods up because the salmon run was poor and the crew would go back to Vancouver earlier. Other reports stated the salmon catches in various seasons and the total number of boxes of canned fish produced for export.

Before leaving at the end of the season, the contractors settled the wages for the crew members and closed the books for the year. The workers would only get their wages after the contractors deducted the housing cost and the expenditure for food. Although the workers were housed in the cannery bunkhouse a small sum of money was deducted as housing costs. Money for food was taken off their paychecks, too. When the books were returned to management, names of the workers were not stated, only the number of persons hired written down. Everyone was given a number for identification. Then contractors told the good and hard-working workers to return for work in the next fishing season but not the slow or poor ones. As the hiring was in the hands of the contractors, some poor workers were called back, especially those who did not complain about the contractors but were willing to spend money purchasing goods from the contractors, according to a retired fish cannery worker.

The End of the Fishing Season

At the end of the fishing season, the native people would go back to their villages[5]. The Chinese workers would return to the lower mainland. Before they packed up for home, both the First Nations people and the Chinese workers wanted to celebrate. The native people usually had a dance festival before they went back to their villages. For the Chinese workers, it was time to give thanks to the All Mighty or Tian Shen before they headed south. In such thanksgiving events the Chinese workers always roasted one or two pigs.

When the Chinese workers came up to the canneries, they always brought a few young pigs. They kept these animals in a pigpen near the bunkhouses or near their vegetable plots, and fed them with slops or leftover food from the mess hall where cannery workers, fishermen and office workers ate. By the end of the canning season, these pigs would be mature and ready for butchering. Once, Walter Wicks, a fisherman who was a teenager living in Port Essington, witnessed a struggle between some Chinese workers and their pig. The Chinese workers strapped the pig on the butchering table and were ready to slaughter it. Somehow the animal managed to get loose and jumped off the table. Four or five Chinese men immediately ran after the escapee. By the time they retrieved the pig they were smeared with dirt and mud[6].

The Activities of the Single Men in their Leisure

Although the Chinese cannery workers lived together as a group and provided companionship for one another, their bond of friendship could not replace the warmth and love of their families. As single men they often felt lonesome and homesick. In a Chinese diary found among the files in a box containing the 1901 fishery reports, the writer described his lonely feelings. Apparently he left his wife shortly after their wedding. In the diary he wrote, "…I could never forget her silky skin and the fragrance given out by her youthful body. Although I met her only on the night of our wedding, I fell in love with her at the very moment I saw her. She was so sweet and gentle…I hope she finds life comfortable living with my parents, and that she has carried out her duty as a good and respectful daughter-in-law. I pray that my parents do not enslave her, but treat her like a daughter…So far I have not received any serious complaints from my parents about her except that she daydreams a lot…In all her letters she reminds me to make lots of money and return home soon. Don't I wish to do that!? I miss her and want to go home to be with her, but when ?…"

In this diary, the writer also recorded the amount of money he earned between August 11 and September 27, 1900. At the back of the diary Cantonese words were used as phonetic for pronouncing some English words. Words like 'good morning,' 'difficult time,' 'day,' 'week,' and others were written in Cantonese dialect for their pronunciation in English. Some useful sentences such as 'I want a dollar a day,' 'You provide transportation and other expenses,' 'You go with me to see the contractor,' were also spelled out in similar fashion. This indicates that the writer attempted to learn and use English. The diary, though written by one cannery worker, reflects the feelings of loneliness and isolation of all the single men who came to fulfill their dreams.

Although the Chinese workers were prepared to work hard, there were days when the catch was small, and they finished their work earlier. In those long summer evenings they often played dominoes, mahjongg, Chinese paper cards (*shiwuhu*) and fan-tan. While these games gave the gamblers some excitement and anticipation, they also resulted in regret and remorse when they lost. Retired Chinese cannery workers say that gambling helped to stimulate their minds, as games like domino and mahjongg require mental strategies and watchfulness in order to win.

When the weather was good, seniors would sit at the doors of their bunkhouses and smoke their favourite pipes while watching a beautiful sunset. Some would go to Dufferrin Street, the main street of the town, to sit or stand around and watch the whites having fun in the bars or saloons. Young Chinese workers usually participated in outdoor recreation. One of their favourite pastimes was tossing a shuttle with the ankles of their feet alternately in an open space.[7] This shuttle is a homemade toy consisting of three large feathers with the shafts inserted into the center of a spool or a stack of rubber washers. The shuttle is tossed into the air by an ankle until the player fails to catch it with the ankle. One person can play this game as a form of exercise, or it can be played by a group in competition to see who can sustain the longest time in tossing, or who can obtain a largest number of tosses within a limited time period; similar to the game of "hackey-sack" that youth play today.

Another favourite outdoor recreation was kite-flying. The *Chock On Fond* collection contains a poem about kite-flying written by a cannery worker. The poem is translated as follows:

> *Though you are sailing*
> *high up in the sky,*
> *you are still held*
> *in my hand.*
> *Fly higher and float afar!*
> *My beloved one*
> *in distant land*
> *would know*
> *I am around*
> *thinking of her,*
> *when she sees*
> *your beautiful wings*
> *fluttering below the clouds.*

Indeed, Chinese people love to fly kites in early autumn when the wind blows. Their kites can be as simple as a piece of quadrangular rice paper pasted on a bamboo frame, or as elaborate as an eagle or butterfly, a real piece of art. It gives the kite maker a sense of great pride when he sees his creation flying high up in the sky. A kite is supposed to be cut off from the string at the end of the windy season, while the kite is still floating in the air. It is a symbol of releasing one's misery or problems.

Mischief and Puzzlement

During the salmon run season, all those who worked in the canneries were very busy except the teenagers who found life routine and monotonous, especially during the summer months. Walter Wicks, a young Canadian, was one of them. At one time a cannery manager reproached him for his poor attitude and mischievous behavior and Wicks wanted to retaliate. He persuaded his friend, the cannery manager's son, to turn off the cannery water supply, without realizing that such action would divert the flow of water to the mess hall. Consequently, a large volume of water flowed through the kitchen floor of the mess hall. That evening, the crew members did not have a meal because the cook had no time to prepare dinners as he had spent his time getting rid of the floodwater.

Another time, when Wicks was hired to pitch salmon from the floor to a butchering bench in one of the canneries, he tossed the fish so high that a Chinese butcher could not catch them. He was told not to do that. Instead, he hurled the next fish higher so that it landed heavily on the neck of the Chinese butcher. In a fit of an anger, the Chinese butcher, holding a knife, chased Wicks out of the cannery and ran after him until he reached the end of a wharf where Wicks jumped into the water. Later, Wicks was pulled out of the water by passersby.[8]

Although the Chinese workers lived and worked with other nationalities in the canneries, their social interactions with others were rather limited. As the Chinese were paid on a piece work basis, they wanted to put in more time in their work in order to get more pay, giving them little time to socialize with others. They also had to contend with racism. The language barrier and cultural differences made it harder for the Chinese to interact with others. Their habits and behavior caused some Canadians to stare at them, especially when they visited the shopping areas in the village. All of them put on identical workman clothing that they bought from Chinese stores in Vancouver or from their contractors. These outfits were grey in color and consisted of pants and tunic.

The pants were held in place with a cord or sash tied around the waist. The tunic was fairly long, coming down to the wearer's thigh. It was open at the centre front with fabric knob and loop fasteners attaching the two front panels together. Some of these tunics had pockets on the front panels. These Chinese working garments were mass-produced and imported from Hong

Kong or Guangzhou. They also wore wooden thongs and put on a dark flannel hat with a narrow rim whenever they went out. Their uniform-like attires made them stand out, especially when they went out in a group. Their dress codes, however, confirmed the fact that the early Chinese population in Canada consisted of mainly men with very few women around to sew for them different fashions of garments, as in China, it was the role of women to make clothing for the family.

Another Chinese habit that puzzled the white people was the way the Chinese workers walked through the streets in Port Essington. When they were on the streets, they always walked in single file as though they were in a parade. This habit was formed when they were in China, as most of them were peasants who used to walk on narrow embankments of their rice fields at home, where it was not possible for them to walk abreast. In Port Essington they might have had to walk in single file because the streets were narrow and many other people went to the center to meet friends and/ or participate in various kinds of activities, especially in the evening. For example, the Salvation Army Band often performed on the street and people usually crowded around to watch their performances.

Greed and Accidents

The Chinese people did not cause the community any trouble or embarrassment, except for two instances.

Two Chinese men were caught stealing from the steamer, *Princess Beatrice*. When the ship docked at Port Essington the two men, who were employees of the steamer, went ashore with the passengers. One was carrying a large suitcase while the other had a gunny sack on his shoulder. The steward of the boat landed on the wharf about the same time as these two men. He pointed them out to a policeman. Upon searching them, the policeman discovered thirty dozen eggs in the suitcase and half a case of quart-sized tins of cream in the gunny sack, taken from the steamer. These two Chinese were sentenced to two months' imprisonment.

Tai Kee, a laundry man, created another Chinese scandal. On June 5, 1909, *The Port Essington Loyalist* reported that Tai Kee had left his premises without paying his employee or returning the laundry to his customers. His employee and customers had hoped that one day he would return to pay them some money, but it did not happen.

Only one incident of accidental death of Chinese cannery workers has been recorded. Two cannery Chinese workers, unaware of the perilous nature of the Skeena, went fishing for halibut. Their small boat was capsized, and the swift current swept them away. When their bodies were discovered, they were buried on a small rocky island off Cunningham Bay in Port Essington. As most of the Chinese people who died in this area were buried there, this island was nicknamed "Chinamen's Island."

"According to a couple of old-timers, some of the bodies were not properly buried there. Some skeletons were found exposed on the island," said Rudolf Jones, a retired CN conductor, familiar with the area. Some people say that Chinese ghosts still haunt this island.

Other Chinese Occupations

There were about five Chinese businessmen living in the fishing village for some years. Old Joe was one of them. Before he opened his restaurant on Dufferin Street, he was a cook in the Cunningham Cannery. After Robert Cunningham sold the cannery, Joe left the company and settled in the village to operate a café. He did good business because people knew him well, and he greeted his customers with smiles and laughter. He was kind and generous to children, who could buy a large quantity of peanuts from him for a nickel. At Halloween he sold firecrackers, and again he gave the children more fire-crackers than their money warranted. Just like all the Chinese people who worked or lived in Port Essington, Joe was a single man. No one knew if he had a family in China, as he seldom left Port Essington.

Around 1915 Lee Yuen opened his restaurant, the New Yick Café, next to Old Joe's on Dufferin Street. In order to attract more customers, he ingeniously designed an illuminated sign, using the light of a kerosene lamp, and hung it at the top of the entrance of his restaurant. The sign, with the words "New Yick Café" written on two glass planes, was supported by a wooden frame. The kerosene lamp was put in between the glass planes. At night when the kerosene lamp was lit, the name of the restaurant could be seen from a distance. Also, he made his own noodles using a traditional Chinese method. Despite his great ideas of promotion and the homemade noodles, Lee Yuen could not compete with Old Joe and shut down the New Yick Café after a year or so.[9]

A couple of Chinese immigrants made their living by carrying water for residents, as drinking water was a problem in Port Essington. Every home had barrels to catch rainwater from the roof or obtained water from a flume connected to a spring on the slope of a nearby hill. In winter, icicles were often knocked down from the eaves of their buildings and melted for house-hold use. During hot, dry summer months the residents went to a distant waterfall to get water. Ah Ging was one of the Chinese water carriers who carried water from the waterfall and sold water to the people at twenty-five cents per bucket.[10]

Lee Wing, the Fish Packer

One would expect to find a few Chinese fishermen in commercial fishing at the coast because the early Chinese immigrants came mainly from the Pearl River (Zhu Jiang) delta in Guangdong Province, where they had been fishermen for centuries. Surprisingly, no record of Chinese fishermen exists except for Lee Wing, the fish packer who moved around between Port Essington, Port Edward and Prince Rupert during his lifetime. A fish packer is the middleman between the fishermen and the canneries. He goes out to the fishing ground to buy and collect fish and then bring the fish back to the cannery.

"The early Chinese immigrants simply could not get into commercial fishing in this country even if they had the skills and fishing experience," said a senior Chinese Canadian in Vancouver. When he was young he worked in the Inverness Cannery for a few summers. "Many of us had to borrow money to pay the head tax when we came. We simply did not have the money to buy a big boat and fishing gear like other fishermen," he continued.

In 1912 Lee Wing came to British Columbia from Guangdong and worked as a cook in the paper and pulp mill at Ocean Falls. Later, he took up a job as a cook in the construction camp of the Grand Trunk Pacific Railway on the opposite bank from Port Essington, then moving to work in the Skeena Commercial Cannery at Port Essington. After some time he went to Smithers and then to Hazelton where he worked as a cook in the community hospitals. At the age of twenty-five, he returned to Port Essington and opened the Skeena Café. His restaurant was well known in town, for he was an excellent cook and always treated his customers generously. He operated the restaurant for a short period and then went back to Guangdong for a visit.

Upon his return, constructed a thirty-one foot boat with the assistance of his Japanese friend, K. Hara. The boat turned out to be three inches wider on one side. Thus, he christened the boat *Kinky*. For many years *Kinky* was used in transporting goods from Prince Rupert to Port Essington. In 1929 he went to work as a chief cook at the Falls River Hydro Project on the Ecstall River.

During his seven months there, he cooked for a crew of 118 people. He then returned to Port Essington and started up the restaurant again. At the same time, he engaged in fish packing and soon became an independent fish packer. He acquired another boat, *Cecil W* and set up his fish camp at

Mawitch Point near the mouth of the Skeena River. He contracted with Nelson Brothers Fisheries to buy fish from a fleet of twenty-four river gillnetters. Equipped with *Kinky* and *Cecil W* and eight other 'contract boats,' he carried out fish packing around the mouth of the Skeena.

As time went by, Lee fell in love with Eileen Dora Wesley, a native girl in Port Essington. They married in 1935, and over the years they produced seven children–Violet, Cecil, Charlotte, Myrtle, Lesley, Harvey and Clarence. Unfortunately, the marriage did not last. In 1946 the couple divorced, leaving Lee to raise the seven children with the help of an occasional nanny.

"Dad was a loving father," said Charlotte Jang, the daughter of Lee Wing. "He always made sure we had enough of everything. Although he was very busy, he attempted to give us Chinese food every day."

"Dad never thought of marrying again after the divorce," continued Jang. "Because we are children of mixed blood, he was afraid that we would not be accepted and treated well by another woman. He preferred to bring us up by himself."

That fear reflects Lee's understanding of the problems facing children of mixed marriages and also his love for his children.

After the divorce, Lee brought the family back to Port Essington where he

Lee Wing - the fish packer - successful business man and loving father.

Photo courtesy Charlotte Jang

bought a general store and a pool room. During the salmon runs, he continued with his fish buying business. When his children went to high school, he found it difficult boarding them in Prince Rupert, so in 1952 he moved his family to Port Edward, which is closer. He bought a home there and started another restaurant business.

"At one time, Lee Wing almost lost his life," said Gladys Blyth, a historian and researcher of the fish canneries on the north coast. " He loved to go beachcombing during his spare time. One day, he was standing on a floating log in a boom near a local sawmill. He slipped and went straight down into the water but popped right up within a few seconds. As he was a heavy person, it took three men nearby to rescue him. When he sank, his pockets were full of coins from the fish buying business, but he did not lose a cent during the accident."

In his later years, Lee's health failed and he stayed in Prince Rupert Hospital for about fourteen years. He passed away in December 1989. One of his sons, Lesley, continued with fish packing for BC Packers after Lee retired from the fish packing business.

The Decline of Port Essington.

In its heyday, Port Essington was a hustle and bustle village. Many people expected that it would develop into an important port or a modern fishing town while maintaining its lumbering and sawmill industries. As time went by, however, it lagged behind, gradually decayed and finally became a ghost town. Many factors contributed to its decline.

Port Essington did not become an important port because ocean liners could not dock in its shallow water. It has little flat land on the beach for building docks or other landing facilities. The turbulent water of the Skeena and the rapids at the Kitselas Canyon claimed many lives in the days when the Skeena was the main waterway. Many canoes were capsized and stern-wheelers sunk in the river. Thus Port Essington did not have the capacity to develop as a transportation centre. The coming of the CNR, which squeezed out water transport, marked the end of any transportation hub ideas they had and the end of Port Essington.

"I have heard reports saying that a canoe, carrying men and loads of gold dust, was capsized in the Skeena in the early days," said Eldon Lee, a doctor in Prince George, who worked in Hazelton in the early 1950s.

"A party of divers came to the Skeena in the 1980s and attempted to salvage some of the lost treasure," recalled Eric Janze, a senior citizen in Hazelton, "but no luck."

By 1920 the number of fish canneries established along the Pacific West Coast and at the mouth of the Skeena had reached about one hundred. As a result, the ocean was over-fished and catches diminished. Some Fishery Department correspondence indicated that it was necessary to revise fishing license regulations and impose more restrictions on commercial fishing. The Department also advocated restoration and conservation programs to maintain the salmon runs in the Skeena region. When the fish cannery industry became fully unionized in the 1940s, the contract system of recruiting Chinese people disappeared. As time went by the population of Port Essington became smaller and smaller. The development of Prince Rupert also attracted canneries to be established on Kaien Island and stimulated the cannery people to leave Port Essington for the more urban centre of Prince Rupert.

Perhaps fire was the final straw in ending Port Essington. Throughout its 90 year history, numerous fires took place. Some of them were very destructive. For example, in 1908 a fire destroyed the Cunningham Sawmill. The estimated loss in the fire was about $25,000. A fire in 1909 burned down two large Chinese bunkhouses. But it was the two fires in the 1960s that truly snuffed out the life of Port Essington. On July 4, 1961, a fire caused by the reflection of light and heat from a broken mirror on a warehouse destroyed most of Port Essington. Within minutes the flames raged through the buildings and board walks, and explosions resulted from the gasoline tanks in fishing boats catching fire. This fire destroyed more than twenty buildings, leaving fifty people homeless.

At that time the total population consisted of approximately one hundred people, but no Chinese. Women and children did not have time to save their belongings, just managing to escape the destructive fire.[11] In 1965 another big fire totally wiped out the remaining townsite. Now Port Essington is a piece of wasteland with charred poles sticking out from the muddy shores while the rising tides ebb quietly, or at times, dash ruthlessly against the rocky terrain.

Chapter Three

THE CASSIAR DISTRICT
&
THE KLONDIKE

The Gold Fever

Whenever someone reported that gold had been found, even if the place was near the Arctic Circle, flanked by snow-capped mountains and deep canyons, or swamps infested with mosquitoes and black flies, miners would flock there. They did not mind wading through swift rivers and stumbling into turbulent rapids to reach the goldfields. The Cassiar Gold Rush was no different when discovered in 1874. Between 1874 and 1895 the official mining reports stated that $4,968,500 of gold was extracted in Laketon, a town on the west side of Dease Lake. Similarly, the production of gold in Dease River, Thibert Creek and McDame Creek also contributed to an equal amount of value in the same period.[1] These reports attracted thousands of miners to the area.

Early Chinese Entry

Numerous news reports, articles and books have indicated that the Chinese people were in the Cassiar District long before the Gold Rush. In 1882 white miners dug up about 30 Chinese brass coins near the bank of a creek. These coins were strung on a piece of wire, which disintegrated after it was exposed to air. The coins remained bright although they looked a little worn. The miners asserted that the ground had not been disturbed by anyone before they dug up the relics. These coins were taken to Victoria for determination of its dates and authenticity. According to some experts in Victoria, these coins were engraved with a date about 1200 BC. Some people speculated that the coins were brought to the District by a group of Chinese sailors, who were

Telegraph Creek in 1920 - one of the Cassiar District's gold rush towns.

BC Provincial Archives

stranded on the west coast of British Columbia after a shipwreck about 3000 years ago.[2]

In 1885, some First Nation people dug up a Chinese vase containing similar Chinese coins. The vase was found entwined in the roots of a huge tree, about three hundred years old. These relics were bronze discs about two inches in diameter with a square hole at the center. On one side of each coin was the symbol of I Ching (Yijing) and on the other side were Chinese ideographs. The ideographs were interpreted by Chinese experts stating that "Heaven is round and the earth is square. The six rules and nine regulations ordain that wherever the spirit of this charm shall visit, all devils shall be exterminated."[3] One of these coins was given to Sun Ming Shu, a County Court interpreter in Victoria when he came up to the Cassiar District to placer mine one summer. Sun presented the charm to Judge Eli Harrison, who sent it to New York and Washington for determination of its date and authenticity. Apparently, Harrison retained the relic until he died, but no one knows who has the coin today.

The presence of these ancient Chinese objects led to speculations about when and who brought to them to Cassiar District. According to the records in Liang Shu (梁书), an ancient Chinese anthology, five Chinese monks and a few of their disciples sailed across the Pacific Ocean en route to the Alaskan coast and reached the west coast of British Columbia around 458 AD. This group of Buddhist devotees, led by Hui Shen (慧深), took forty-one years to complete their round trip from China to the Pacific Coast of North America and back. Apparently they sailed along the warm Japanese ocean current to the north and then down south along the Pacific Coast of North America before they followed the equatorial ocean current to sail home. Hui Shen was the only monk to return to China. No one knows what had happened to the other four or their disciples. They may have died on the journey or remained in North America.

Upon his return, Hui gave an account of the countries he visited to several court historians who recorded his discoveries. One of his descriptions stated that he had visited a place about 20,000 Li, approximately 9700 kilometers, east of China. He called this place "Fusang" (扶桑) where red mulberry trees grew profusely. "Fu" means 'help' or 'nurturing' in Chinese and "sang" refers to the red mulberry trees. Putting these two words together the term "Fusang" means helping the people in the red mulberry land. In his narrative Hui Shen asserted that the five monks had attempted to deliver the teaching of Buddha to the native tribes as a means of helping these people to attain salvation. The following excerpt is translated from Liang Shu:

> ...On the land of Fusang, the red mulberry plants
> produced oval-shaped leaves similar to *paulownia*
> and edible purplish red fruits. The place was rich
> in copper and traces of gold and silver but no iron.
> The native tribes in Fusang were civilized, living
> in well-organized communities. They produced paper
> from the bark of the red mulberry plants for writing
> and produced cloth from the fibers of the bark. Their
> houses or cabins were constructed with red mulberry
> wood. The fruits and young shoots of the plants were
> one of their food sources. They raised deer for meat
> and milk, just as the Chinese raised cattle at home,
> and produced cheese with deer milk. They traveled
> on horseback and transported their goods with carts
> or sledges pulled by horses, buffalo or deer.

...An emperor, or a main chief, with the help of
several officials, governed the country. The majority of
people were law-abiding citizens. The country had no
army or any military defense but two jails, one in north
and the other in south of the country. Those who had
committed serious crimes were sent to the north jail
and they stayed there for their entire lives. These
inmates, however, could get married. If they got
married and produced children, their sons
became slaves and daughters remained as maids
in the community.
...The marriage arrangement was relatively simple.
If a boy wanted to marry a girl, he had to build a
cabin next to the home of the girl and
stay there for a year. If the girl liked him they
would get married; otherwise he would be asked
to go away.
...When a person died in the community
his body would be cremated. The mourning period
varied from seven days for the death of a parent to
five days for a grandparent and three days for a
brother or sister. During their mourning period they
were not supposed to consume food, only water. They
had no religion.

Hui Shen and his fellow monks attempted to preach Buddhism to these
people while traveling through the country. Wherever they went, they left
behind images of Buddha and literature of Buddhism for the people.[4] This
account of Fusang, which was also translated by a couple of Jesuit priests at
the turn of the century, aroused the interest and curiosity of a number of
historians. From the descriptions of the flora and fauna, and the mineral
deposits, some historians like John Murray Gibson, John Windsor and A.B.
McKelvie have suggested that Fusang was a place in British Columbia's
northwest, as some of the customs described were similar to the native practices there.

Whether the monks had visited the Cassiar District and deposited the
coins in the locations mentioned above, is a subject worthy of further inves-
tigations. The discovery of the ancient Chinese coins indicates that Chinese
people may have been in this country much earlier than previously thought.

Chinese Gold Miners

"At the beginning of the Gold Rush, the early Chinese in the Cassiar region were forced to leave," said Diane Smith, a manager of the Atlin Historical Society. "They were eventually allowed to mine in the Cassiar creeks after the rush was over. By then no one complained about the presence of Chinese any more. The Chinese miners were meticulous in mining their claims. Miners, who came across some Chinese old claims years afterward, soon realized that it was pointless to re-work those claims because the Chinese miners had worked on their claims so thoroughly that nothing would be left."

The names of Chinese miners and Chinese mining companies first appeared in the gold commissioner's records in 1879, a few years after the peak of the Gold Rush. Between 1879 and 1883, about thirty Chinese placer miners were issued with mining certificates in Cassiar District. The Chinese mining companies such as Mah Sing, Lee Hong, Sing Cum Yun, the Wrangel owned by Ho Kow, and the Rath owned by Hop Yun, were found in the vicinity of Thibirt Creek. The Discovery and Lee Company, owned by Lee Duck Wong and Do Foo, were in Depot Creek. Between 1891 and 1901, Yep Sing and Company as well as other Chinese miners such as Ah Cow, Book

The Warburton Pike's Hydraulic Mine at Thibert Creek in 1912

BC Provincial Archives

Ching, Duck Sing, Mong Sing and Yee Wah, registered their claims in the vicinity of McDavis Creek. All these Chinese miners were single men and camped out on their claims during summer. In winter, they went to Telegraph Creek, Laketon or McDame Creek. Others went to Hazelton or Juneau during off-season. All of them lived a lonely and isolated life but they were focused mainly on the chances of striking it rich.

The gold commissioner's casebook registered many requests and complaints from the Chinese miners, similar to those of the white miners. Their requests included asking permission to build wing-dams on certain creeks or streams, so that they could get to the bedrock, or to dig drains through their properties to get rid of excess water. Wing-dams were piles of rocks to divert or regulate the flow of water of a creek. They are usually erected in early spring when the water level of the creek is low. Many wing-dams still remain in various mining areas.

Complaints consisted of allegations that other miners had jumped their claims or cleared out their sluice boxes while they were away. Other complaints stated that the tailing or mud and gravel of the adjacent mine had spilled over their mining ground, covering up the land. Some asserted that the spill-over had filled up the creek beds. Therefore, there was no water to pan gold or to operate their hydraulic pumps and sluice boxes. These complaints reveal the greed and suspicions of miners during all the Gold Rushes.

On June 19, 1878, the gold commissioner recorded a dispute between Ho Kow, the owner of the Wrangel Company, and Lee Leong, a foreman of the Rath Company, at Thibert Creek. Lee diverted a creek from its natural course causing flooding in the mining claim of the Wrangel Company. Ho admitted that Lee had informed him of the action, but he had suggested Lee build a wing-dam to regulate the flow of water, so that the Wrangel mining property would not be affected. Lee, however, did not want to build the wing-dam because too much work would be involved. He told Ho that he was willing build the dam if Ho would give a lending hand. In court, Lee asserted that Ho had given him permission for turning the course of the creek. Ho denied having given permission and stressed that he only agreed to the request on condition that Lee would build a wing-dam.

During the court session, a witness, Thomas LeForist, claimed that he had warned Lee not to carry out such a venture, because the water would not only drown the Wrangel Company's property but also flood the Ming Star Company's mine. LeForist was the owner of the Ming Star Company, whose mining land was adjacent to the Wrangel Company's claim. He offered to assist Lee in building a wing dam, but Lee was not interested in building it. Hop Yun, the owner of the Rath Company, was another witness in the case. He had employed Lee to operate the mine in the disputed area. In court Hop claimed that he went to inspect the area after the course of creek had been diverted. He spoke to Ho at the first sign of flooding. Ho had not complained about the water at that time. When more water drained into Ho's property, Hop suggested that both the Wrangel Company and the Rath Company work together to fix the damage, but Ho disagreed. In the end the court decided that the Rath Company had caused the damage and had to fix the wreckage. Lee had to pay Ho $30.50 for the loss.

On the same day another dispute between Peter Farrel and Ah Foong was tried in the Cassiar County Court, when Farrel filed a suit for relief from an injunction. In this case, Ah Foong asserted that Farrel had jumped his claim at Thibert Creek. In court, Farrel presented his cause as follows. In August of the previous year, Farrel went to the ground at Thibert Creek. Having noticed no fresh stake on the said property, he applied for licence at the Government agency to work on one hundred feet of the ground. He worked there for about two weeks and no one came out to make any claim on the mining ground. In the third week, Ah Foong came to the property and told Farrel that it belonged to him. Farrel asked Foong to show him the required papers, but Foong could not produce them on the spot. Farrel continued working on the land for about eight more days, and then he went away to work for the Rath Company for a week or so.

He returned to his ground and worked for another ten more days before the weather got too cold. He applied for leave of absence before he left the claim, and he asked his friend Danny Crad to post the notice of his absence on the claim for him. Upon his return on June 7 the next year, Farrel received an injunction from the court stating that he was working illegally on Ah Foong's claim. This action took place four days before Farrel's licence expired. Farrel had not realized that he had to renew his licence ahead of time. He assumed that he could continue working on the ground because the secretary of the Government agency had the previous record.

During the trial Farrel appealed to have the injunction removed. He said that, from the time he applied for the ground to the day he left for winter, he did not see any Chinese miners working in the area. He asserted that if the Chinese miner was around, he would have noticed him. Further, Foong should have been able to see his leave of absence notice posted on the claim.

Patrick Smith, another witness and employee of the Bright Star Company, testified that he had seen only Farrel working in the area. The Bright Star's property was above the claim in dispute. He claimed that he had posted the leave of absence for Farrel on behalf of Danny Crad. He declared that he did not see Ah Foong on the ground until June 18 of that year.

Dennis Creek, another witness, who worked close to the ground in dispute, said that he noticed only Farrel working on the ground but not Ah Foong. He asserted that he would notice any Chinese miner in the area because his claim was only about 300 feet away. His property was on the same level with the ground in dispute. Unfortunately, Ah Foong's testimony was missing. The court case ended with the removal of the injunction and Farrel was allowed to hold the 100 feet of ground as recorded by him.

On August 6, 1878 another similar dispute took place between Fidell Bumillar and Ah Foong, the employee of the Sing Cum Yun Company at Thibirts Creek. In this court case, Bumillar was not relieved from the injunction, and Ah Foong was allowed to hold the claim.

Some Chinese miners were brought to court because they did not pay their debts. On December 16, 1879, Fletcher & Company accused that Ah You had not paid the company the $150 that he owed them. Ah You declared that he had no money to pay his debts. He said that men, who owed him money at McDavis Creek, left the area without paying him. Consequently, he had no money to pay his creditors. Ah Ling, a witness, testified that he had paid Ah You $150 before he left McDavis Creek and believed that Ah You had paid $50 to Wright and Company, one of Ah You's creditors. The final judgment was against Ah You, who had to pay $78.55 to Fletcher & Company, and $27.50 as fees to the court.

Another small debt claim dealt with transportation costs for supplies. Apparently Yee Wah did not pay Gaulraith G.H.K, a pack-train company, for delivering goods to him at Laketon. In this case, the court ruled that Yee Wah had to pay the pack-train company $286.06 for the goods and freight, and $114.50 to the court.

There were numerous cases involved with labour disputes. In one case, Ah Chin and his associates had to pay labourers at Carter and Wilson a sum of $ 198.50 and $6.50 to the court. Between 1878 and 1879, at least twelve Chinese miners and eight Chinese mining companies were involved in mining disputes and small debt claims with others, including both Chinese and whites. These small debt claims and disputes indicated not all miners got rich in mining. Some of them were so poor that they could not make ends meet. These cases also revealed the dark side of human nature, that there are people who cheat on others, if given a chance.

In the gold commissioner's casebook, Hong Lai, owner of a Chinese general and grocery store at Laketon, had sued a number of miners, both Chinese and white, for non-payment of mining supplies and provisions purchased from his store. In these cases, Hong Lai managed to recover most of the money. The fact that Hong Lai had established a Chinese general store in Laketon suggests that a good number of Chinese miners were in the Cassiar District, as generally speaking, Chinese stores were set up only when there were sufficient numbers of Chinese miners around. These stores brought in provisions such as rice, salt fish and other Chinese food items and would not be able to make a profit if there were few Chinese. These incidents, good or bad, disclose the difficult lives of gold miners, both white and Chinese[5]. To many of them, gold mining was the dream of getting rich so they could carry on their lives somewhere else.

At the beginning of the Cassiar Gold Rush when most of the Chinese men were chased out, one Chinese cook, name unknown, was allowed to stay. He was commended for the good deeds he performed for others. During winter this Chinese cook provided meals for many miners when food was scarce, and is credited for saving men from starvation. "One episode stays in my mind," Diane Smith remarked. "He was feeding those men who chased his fellowmen out of the area. I believe he later lived in Juneau, Alaska, where Chinese miners were also chased out. But, like the unknown cook in Cassiar, cooks provided an important service to the miners and were no threat to the job market. The Cassiar cook would have found safe, profitable work in Juneau among white miners who already knew and respected him."

Ah Clem, another well known Chinese, gained honor and respect around Telegraph Creek. A bend on the Stikine River, some distance north of Telegraph Creek, is called Ah Clem Point. Whatever he did for others and his own achievements is unknown. However, the fact that a place is named after him suggests he had influence and respect in the area. In the following photograph he sits side by side with a white man at the entrance of a cabin. They appear very much at ease with each other.

In 1923, a second discovery of gold took place in the Cassiar District. Once again, white miners flocked to the region. Some anticipated that the colorful life of Telegraph Creek would be revived, but the dream was short-lived. For this period, no information about Chinese mining activities is available. This occurrence is not surprising, as that very year the Chinese Exclusion Act was passed, prompting many Chinese immigrants to congregate themselves in the lower mainland. In larger cities they could get protection and support from their clan organizations and from various Chinese benevolent associa-

Left: Joe Williams, trapper
Right: Ah Clem, a well respected
Chinese resident in Telegraph
Creek - 1900s.

BC Provincial Archives

tions. They were afraid of assaults and violence in areas where the whites greatly out-numbered them.

Klondike - The Forbidden Frontier

Very few people have *not* heard of the Klondike Gold Stampede in 1898. Naturally, Chinese miners wanted to go to the Klondike to find their fortune just like everyone else. However, the Caucasian miners successfully excluded them. The Caucasian miners declared openly that they wanted to keep the Yukon Territory to themselves. At that time, the anti-Chinese sentiment was simmering throughout the whole province, and white Canadians were making every effort to exclude Chinese immigrants from getting into any job market. In the new territories occupied mainly by Caucasians, it was not difficult for them to stop Chinese immigrants from migrating there. Although the laws did not permit anyone to resort to assault and violence, white people could find other ways to make the Chinese feel unwanted. The following episode describes how the whites managed to exclude the Chinese from reaching the Yukon Territory.

Four Chinese immigrants from Victoria ventured north. One of them could speak English and was able to communicate with the whites, therefore, they thought they would have a better chance to stay in the north, so long as they did not cause any problems. In June, 1902 these men arrived at Whitehorse on their way to Dawson City. The news of their coming reached Whitehorse just before they did. The community immediately formed a city council and elected Jack West as mayor.

At the first meeting, the council discussed strategies to stop the Chinese men from going any farther. When the Chinese arrived at Whitehorse, West and his council members met them and escorted them to a vacant lot. West and the council told the Chinese to erect a tent and spend the night there as no hotel in Whitehorse would accommodate them. West gave them some 'fatherly' advice and told them to take the next train back to where they came from. He reminded them that the next train going south would be leaving the next day at 9:00 a.m. West and his council members made it very clear to the Chinese that "they would never have any friends in the Yukon Territory and it was good for them to get out as soon as they got the chance."[6] The Chinese miners, however, were determined to go to Dawson City and did not want to return to Victoria. The council wanted to use force to expel the Chinese from the area but the RCMP wouldn't allow it. West went back to the Chinese and urged them to go home.

The Chinese then told him that they did not have any money to buy their return tickets, but West and his council told them that it was a criminal offense to enter the Yukon Territory without money. The Chinese attempted to ignore the threat and pretended that they could not understand what was being said. However, when the train arrived the next morning, the Chinese men were shuffled on board and the issue of their having no money was forgotten. Hence, the people in Yukon were able to keep their territory free of Chinese miners.

Chinese miners did arrive in the Cassiar District, but their time there was short-lived. However, their presence there is part of the tapestry of northern history. As Diane Smith remarks, "It should be gathered before it fades away completely."

Chapter Four

PRINCE RUPERT I

The Rainbow City

The sky above Prince Rupert, the most important port in northwestern British Columbia, is often dark and cloudy with shrouds of mist hovering above its harbour. It is common to find pedestrians wearing rain gear, as during the rainy season very few people use an umbrella because it can act as a parachute, lifting the umbrella holder up into the air when a strong wind blows. At times, the thick clouds separate and beams of sunlight penetrate. When the mist or drizzle reflects the sunlight, a rainbow appears, a common occurrence in Prince Rupert, hence its name, Rainbow City.

The city, named after King Charles II's cousin Prince Rupert and incorporated in 1910, is located at Tuck's Inlet on Kaien Island near the mouth of the Skeena River. Nearby Digby Island shelters the inlet, the warm Japanese ocean current keeping it free from ice in winter and the deep water allowing ocean liners to use it throughout the year. An excellent port, Prince Rupert is connected to the mainland and nearby islands by the Yellowhead Highway and the CNR. These transport systems deliver Canadian products such as lumber, paper, pulp, coal, wheat, and fish to Prince Rupert for export to the Pacific Rim. Prince Rupert has an airport at Digby Island and offers float plane services to the nearby communities from Seal Cove. BC Ferries connect it to the Queen Charlotte Islands and to Port Hardy on Vancouver Island.

The Early Chinese Immigrants

On May 17, 1906, the steamer, *Constance*, landed at Tuck Inlet and brought a group of surveyors, engineers, axemen, carpenters and a Chinese cook to Kaien Island. They were there to survey the land for a job constructing the railway terminus. When Prince Rupert was selected to be the Grand Trunk

Pacific Railway (GTP) terminus, Chinese immigrants from all over settled there. Numerous Chinese names such as Willie Lung, Lee Yick, Tom Fong, Lee Jew, Jip Sam, Ki Wing and Chinese companies like King Tai, Hop Lee and others were noted in the newspapers of the early days. The King Tai Company obtained contracts from the GTP to clear land and produce railroad ties for the railway construction.

Nothing much else has been documented about the early Chinese immigrants except for the crimes that some of them committed. Willie Lung, a Chinese doctor in Metlakatla, was caught selling liquor to natives. He was fined $100.00 plus $ 7.50 in court costs. Lee Jew, Jip Sam and Ki Wing were found guilty of possessing opium illegally and were fined $50 each.[1]

On June 12, 1909, the *Prince Rupert Empire* openly advocated the policy of not employing the non-Asiatic in public works, businesses and industries, a policy spearheaded by the Vancouver Trade and Labour Council. In one of its editorials, the *Prince Rupert Empire* complained aloud that GTP had given a Chinese laundry man permission to locate at Prince Rupert but refused to give a white laundry man the same privilege. Between 1909 and 1911 several articles and letters to the editor appeared in the *Prince Rupert Empire* urging the general public to boycott the Chinese laundry business. They accused Chinese laundry men of employing the unhygienic method of spraying water from their mouths on dry clothing before they ironed it. This practice meant germs from the mouths of the Chinese men would spread on the garments and lodge on the rough edges of shirt collars. It was a dangerous practice which should be stopped, said Dr. Herman Spaldin, the health officer in charge of contagious diseases.

Other Caucasian laundry business took advantage of the complaints and turned the allegations into a form of advertisement for their businesses. In 1911, the Pioneer Laundry owned and operated by white Canadians, advertised in the *Prince Rupert Daily News* with a cartoon depicting a Chinese laundry man spraying the water from his mouth on the clothing. The captions of the cartoon wrote: "Do away with this [spraying water with mouth]. Patronize a white laundry. White labour only at Pioneer Laundry. Phone 118". The advertisement appeared in the newspaper for more than a year.

Similarly, the newspaper accused GTP of favoring a Chinese immigrant to set up a bakery shop, forcing the white men and women to eat sourdough bread made by Chinese cooks. At that time the anti-Chinese movement in British Columbia was at it's peak. Thomas D. Patullo, a member of the Liberal Party, expressed his concerns about hiring Chinese immigrants in the lumber industry. He feared that the lumber industry might get into the hands of the Orientals as the fish industry had. He reminded the forest industry to honour the clause in the licenses that Orientals should be employed in limited numbers.[2]

In a slight change of heart, however, the newspaper printed an editorial stating that it was ludicrous that the Grand Trunk Inn, owned by GTP Company, had employed a Chinese cook, and yet refused accommodation for a Chinese land speculator from Vancouver when he went to Prince Rupert to look at his properties. The editorial stated that all travelers, whether they be Asiatic or European, were entitled to accommodation at a public hotel.

In 1920, seven Chinese names, Kwong Sang Hing, Kwong High Chong, Kwong Sun Chong, Cheng Foong, Chow Sing, Lee Wong and Wing Ching Yen were found in the phone directory. Three of them were listed as cooks working for Cheng Chong & King Tai Company. Presumably Cheng Chong & King Tai was a railroad-tie producing company with living quarters that provided food for its employees. Some Chinese businesses, including the Prince Rupert Grocery, the Sunrise Grocery, the Hop Lee Company, the Lew Lunn Company, the Wong Laundry and the Lew Yee Laundry were found in the court records of small debt claims. Between 1924 and 1940, King Tai Company had eight cases against its debtors and recovered large sums of money.[3] These businesses no longer exist or have had their names changed.

The Mah family

Among the early immigrants, Mah Boon Kuan was one of the few who made his mark in Prince Rupert. Mah immigrated to British Columbia with his wife and son, Edward Mah Chung Gee. They first settled at Rossland in 1910. They also brought with them a maid from China. That the whole family, including a maid, came to Canada indicates that the Mah family had been wealthy in China. The presence of the maid exhibits some old customs of rich Chinese homes. During the Qing dynasty when the daughter of a wealthy family got married, her parents usually bought her a maid. After the wedding the bride usually lived with her husband and in-laws for her entire life. The maid would follow the bride and serve her mistress in the new home. The maid worked for her owner until she reached her late teens, when her mistress would then find her a husband. Unlucky maids who did not marry would remain as servants to their mistresses for their entire life.

In Rossland, Mah was popular in the Chinese community because he could read and write Chinese characters as well as being knowledgeable in English.

Since he was a learned man, he automatically became the interpreter for the Chinese immigrants there.

"Grandpa used to read newspapers to the Chinese people in a restaurant at Rossland when he was young. At that time the Chinese people always wanted to know what was happening in China as well as in Canada," said Patricia Mah. There was a good reason for their interest.

At the turn of the 20th century, there was a nationalism movement in China that aimed at overthrowing the Qing Dynasty. Chinese people around the world were anxious to know about the events in China. Not only did most of them still have families there, they had been taught from an early age that Chinese people should put the well-being of their country ahead of everything, including their families. Therefore, the situation in China was important to them. The Chinese immigrants in Rossland turned to Mah to tell them the news about China since many of them could not read or write.

While in Rossland, Mah came across advertisements about Prince Rupert, which claimed that the town would be a modern metropolis like New York, a busy trading center with skyscrapers, first class hotels, broad streets, gardens and parks. It would, trumpeted the posters, become an important port to the Orient since it was 500 miles or 800 kilometers closer to Asia than Vancouver. With visions of a towering northern city in his head, Mah, his family and a friend decided to move to Prince Rupert. They arrived in 1912.

At first, Mah worked for the King Tai Company to learn logging and how to produce railroad ties. Later, he began his own business producing railroad ties. On May 25, 1912, his second son, Earl, was born, the first Chinese baby in Prince Rupert. Two more children, Alec and Lily, were eventually added to the family. According to Chinese custom, men were allowed to marry more than one wife and have concubines if they could afford to do so. Consequently, Mah took a second wife in Canada who bore seven more children for him. Two of these children, Albert and Cedric, were well-known pilots in World War II.

In 1920, Mah opened the Sunrise Grocery store at the corner of Fulton street and Sixth Avenue. Many senior citizens, both white and Chinese, remember his kindness and generosity towards his customers. He trusted his customers and often gave them credit. When the customers paid their bill on time, he usually rewarded them with a basket of fruit or chocolates. Soon the Sunrise Grocery was doing a thriving business and its customers included people from Port Simpson, Alice Arm, Kincolith, Stewart, Cedervale, Skeena Crossing and the lighthouse stations along the north coast. During the early 1930s, Mah showed his caring spirit to the residents in Prince Rupert. No needy person would be turned away when he or she came to get food. At Christmas every customer got a turkey as a gift.

Mah died in 1935. Like most Chinese immigrants, he wanted to be buried in his family plot in Taishan, China. His second wife and their seven children together with Mah Boon Chuck, Mah's cousin, took the remains back for burial. Mah Boon Chuck, known as San Gong, meaning the third grand uncle to the younger generation, was required to return with the family because he knew how to organize Chinese funeral rituals.

"At that time my grandmother and my mother Lily were in China," said Jack Wong, a grandson. His grandmother was Mah's first wife. "Both of them went back to Taishan in 1929. When the body of my grandpa arrived home, most of the family members were there already."

"My father Earl was there too," added Patricia Mah. "He went home to build a bigger house for the family before grandpa passed away."

After the funeral, all the boys and two girls returned to Prince Rupert, leaving the two wives and three daughters in China. Edward, Earl and Alec took over Sunrise Store. Albert and Cedric and two younger sisters continued their education in Prince Rupert. Two years later, Albert and Cedric went to California to take up aviation lessons. In 1942, Earl and Alec bought the Prince Rupert Bakery, leaving Edward to operate the Sunrise Store. Today, Mah's surviving children are either living in the lower mainland or in other provinces. Some of his grandchildren and great-grandchildren still live in Prince Rupert.

The First Chinese Alderman

Earl Mah, the second son of Mah Boon Kuan also made his mark in Prince Rupert. It is not an exaggeration to state that almost every resident of Prince Rupert, in the past or present, has heard of Earl. The Aquatic Center in Prince Rupert is dedicated to him for his service to the community. As he was born in Prince Rupert, he attended the Borden Street School, and after graduation he not only helped out in his father's business but also was involved in community activities. He was an active member of the Rotary Club, and a director of the Prince Rupert Tourist Bureau as well as the director of the Friendship House. He was interested in politics and became a lifetime member of the Social Credit Party. At one time he was the vice-president of the BC Social Credit Party.

As mentioned previously, Earl became the sole owner of the Prince Rupert Bakery and operated the business until he retired in 1975, when he leased it to his daughter Patricia and his son-in-law Paul Mar. The store burnt down in 1982 but was rebuilt in 1984. Now it is known as the Baker's Boy.

After Earl retired from business in 1975, he became involved in municipal politics and was elected as an alderman of Prince Rupert City Council in 1977. "Dad felt that the community had nurtured him, and he should serve and contribute something to the community in return," said Pat Mah.

In January 1977, the *Prince Rupert Daily News* stated that for the first time in the history of the city, a member of the Chinese community took office as alderman on city council. After serving the city council for two years, he retired from politics because of his poor health. On August 17, 1979, Mayor Lester of Prince Rupert presented Earl with a plaque in recognition of his service to the city. He died on July 29, 1981, survived by his wife, Lillian, three sons, two daughters, ten grandchildren, six brothers and four sisters.

The Flying Tigers

Both younger sons of Mah Boon Kuan, Albert and Cedric, were famous Chinese pilots from Prince Rupert. Albert is well-known for his interesting and daring feat of getting Bernice, his youngest sister, out of China during the Japanese occupation.

After the death of his father, Mah Boon Kuan, his mother and three younger sisters did not return to Canada. These women were stranded in China during World War II because communication between them and their relatives in Prince Rupert was cut off. The Mahs in Prince Rupert could not send any money home after the Japanese occupied Guangdong. By 1943, Mrs. Mah Boon Kuan had sold all her jewelry and valuable belongings. They were almost living in starvation because of the inflation during war time. At that time, both Albert and Cedric were teaching in the British Commonwealth Training Air Program in Manitoba. Somehow, Albert learned about the destitute situation of his mother and sisters. Immediately, he applied for compassionate leave and joined the China National Aviation Corporation (CNCA) so that he could find his way to reach his mother and sisters.

In early 1944, he took a plane from Calcutta across the mountainous border to reach Guilin in the Province of Guangxi, which is northwest of Guangdong. From there he went by train and then by boat to Liuzhou where he spent a night with a friend. The next day he boarded a large junk pulled by a tugboat and sailed along the Zhu Jiang River to the its delta. The junk stopped at Wuzhou where he had to find other transportation to take him to his village Fei-E Chun in Taishan county.

Cedric Mah (left) and Albert Mah (right), known as the Prince Rupert Flying Tigers.
Prince Rupert Museum & Archives

While traveling in the junk he met Elsa, a Chinese girl who was on her way home from New York University in the United States. After learning about his mission, Elsa introduced him to her uncle in a letter. Her uncle was a rice and wine merchant in Kongmoon (Jiangmen). She told her uncle to help Albert find the way to Taishan. When he arrived at Jiangmen, he was in his CNCA uniform. Elsa's uncle was surprised to find him safe and sound. At that time the Guomindang party was the enemy of both the Japanese and the Communists. The CNAC uniform would identify him as a member of the Guomindang party. Bandits and robbers in the country had no regard for members of the Guomindang either, they usually took away money or belongings of any Guomindang members. Nevertheless, Elsa's uncle made arrangements for Albert to reach Fei-E Chun. He also hired two coolies, at a rate of 2000-yuan (Chinese currency) per day to help Albert with his luggage and to accompany him on his journey.

It took Albert and his escorts five days to arrive at Fei-E Chun. This part of his journey sounds like fiction but is true. The first day of his journey he walked until his boots wore off. The next day he rode on a bicycle but the chain kept falling off. On the following two days, the coolies carried him in a coffin to avoid being captured by Japanese and then on a sedan chair while traveling through the narrow ridges of paddy fields. On the fifth day they arrived at Pak Sha Ngan (Bai Sha Yan), a town near his village. On the way to his village the two coolies conspired to kill him because they wanted the large sum of money he had with him. Upon hearing their conversation, he jumped off the sedan chair. He put one hand in one of his pockets in such a manner that it appeared like he had a gun. He pointed at them and then ordered the coolies to lead the way. The coolies thought that he would kill them if they disobeyed, so they trotted ahead of him. Finally he reached home. His mother and sisters were overjoyed when they saw him. The coolies, however, wanted more money but were paid according to their agreement and were dismissed.

The situation in the village was pitiful and horrifying. Many people had no money to buy food and were eating roots, bark and leaves from trees. Some resolved to bully, rob or even kill one another to stay alive. A few turned to cannibalism and ate human flesh. Once, his mother bought some rice, but villains in the village took it away from her. Japanese guards could not control the situation for the peasants killed the Japanese when they attempted to interfere.[5]

After Albert arrived in China, he made plans to take the family back to Prince Rupert. However, it was not safe for all of them to leave together. Eventually, Albert decided to take Bernice, his 12 year old sister, with him first. Before he left, he gave his mother a large sum of money and also made arrangements with some friends in China to send money to his mother regularly, so that the family would not go hungry again.

His return trip with his sister was as dramatic as his trip to China. While they were sailing on the Zhu Jiang, several enemy planes, Japanese Zeros, chased them. Both the tugboat and the junk were forced to land. In Guilin, they boarded an overloaded train that failed to climb a slight grade. Passengers came down and pushed the train forward. Guilin fell into the hands of the Japanese soon after they left and so, Albert and Bernice took a detour to Chung King (Chong Qing) where they figured out how to get to Calcutta. After arriving in Calcutta, Bernice stayed with a friend while Albert made arrangements to get her back to Prince Rupert. Meanwhile, Albert had returned to serve in the CNAC. After several months, Albert was able to take Bernice to Bombay where they could take a boat back to North America. Again it took days before Bernice was finally on her way, but on the day of departure Albert was prohibited from accompanying Bernice to the pier. As the ship left, he realized that Bernice did not have a passport or any document with her to indicate that she was originally from Canada. Quickly he wired a friend in New York asking him to look out for Bernice and to help her to land in United States when the ship docked. Months passed. There was no sign of Bernice having arrived at New York. The boat had taken her to California where she was kept in an immigration jail at San Pedro. It took days to check her identity. Bernice arrived in Prince Rupert after World War II ended.[6]

These events demonstrate a strong bond of love and care between Albert and his family. It highlights the dangers in traveling during wartime as well as China's devastating conditions during Japanese occupation.

Cedric Mah, too, has many wartime stories to tell. After he had obtained his aviation diploma in California, he returned to Canada to fly bush planes between Winnipeg and Edmonton. In 1943 he joined the CNAC. His job was to transport emergency supplies from India to China in the war. After the Japanese cut off Burma Road, the airline was the only connection between China and the outside world. Flying from India over the Himalayas to China was a most dangerous route to take. The mountain ranges, whose lofty peaks were capped with permanent ice, have been nicknamed as the "humps" and the pilots who flew over the mountains in that route were known as the "humpty dumpties." The weather over the humps is often stormy and unpredictable during the monsoons. Many pilots have lost their lives within the ranges. Although Cedric had flown over the humps many times, he was almost one of them.

Immediately after WWII, he was assigned to carry six bags of newly minted Chinese currency, weighing about 5000 kilograms, to the Bank of China in Shanghai. When he was over the humps, one of the engines failed and a wing froze with ice. In order to save the lives of his crew, he had to jettison much of the heavy money. Having done that, he slowly landed his plane in the lower altitudes of the humps. Once he deiced the plane, he resumed his journey. To this day, the money is still lying somewhere in the Himalayan Mountains.[7]

In 1950, he returned to Canada and continued his flying career as a bush pilot. He has now retired from flying, but his love of flying saved many lives and has earned the gratitude of many people. As one example, in 1980 a private plane crashed into a glacier on Mt. Waddington.[8] Cedric came to the rescue. Travelling to the accident site, he repaired the plane and flew it over the Rockies to bring it home safely in Campbell River. Albert and Cedric were known as the Flying Tigers for their flying adventures during WWII and their exploits as bush pilots. They certainly left a page of colorful history in Prince Rupert.

Chinese Workers in the Fish Industry

According to the Salmon Cannery Pack Statistics, seven fish canneries were found on Kaien Island near the vicinity of Prince Rupert. The first cannery was the Tuck's Inlet Cannery, with its fish and cold storage facilities constructed at Seal Cove in 1913. Details about the Chinese involvement in this cannery are missing. Although there is no historical record, one can assume that they were employed in this cannery and carried out tasks similar to those of the Chinese cannery workers at Port Essington. The introduction of an "Iron Chink" into the cannery at Tuck's Inlet in 1923 is further evidence of Chinese workers being employed there.

At that time, most canneries were attempting to replace Chinese workers with machinery and later with First Nations workers. This management strategy certainly affected the Chinese workers in the fish canneries. For example, the North Pacific Cannery at Port Edward, about 13 kilometers south of Prince Rupert, employed only 44 Chinese and 140 First Nations workers in 1944[9]. Six other fish canneries–the Babcock, the Oceanside, Prince Rupert Nelson Brothers, Seal Cove, Prince Rupert Co-op and the Royal–were established in Prince Rupert between 1940 and 1962.

After World War II, the fish industries unionized and the Chinese contract system was gradually phased out. Some canneries still retained their Chinese Bosses to recruit manpower for the canneries. Since the Bosses had been in the trade for some time, they would be able to find hard-working and reliable workers for the canneries. By then the roles of the China Bosses had changed; they were required only to recruit Chinese workers and supervise them in their work. As the Chinese workers were union members, they received their wages directly from the company, not from the contractors.

After 1948, the Family Reunion Immigration Act allowed Chinese Canadians to sponsor their immediate family members to Canada. Many Chinese Canadians in Prince Rupert sent for their families. Some of these new immigrants, who arrived in the 1950s, went to work in the canneries during the fishing season. These cannery workers did not live in cannery bunkhouses, as most of them had their families in Prince Rupert. Chinese women, too, took up casual work as fish cleaners and can fillers. Although the number of Chinese increased, the majority chose not work in the canneries.

Large numbers of seasonal workers from Vancouver still traveled to the north coast to work at the Port Edward, Inverness, North Pacific, and Sunnyside canneries. These workers stayed in the company bunkhouses, but life for these workers was less lonely for they could go to Prince Rupert where many Chinese restaurants, grocery stores and other business had already been established. Also, their work schedule had changed; they were no longer required to work for fifteen-to-sixteen-hours-a-day as they were not paid by the number of fish they could butcher or the number of cans of fish they could produce. They were union members and worked in shifts. On their days off, they usually came to Prince Rupert, thus making the city a social gathering place for both the Chinese Canadians and Chinese immigrants.

"We were told that some of the Chinese cannery workers from Port Edward, North Pacific and other canneries often came to Prince Rupert to shop, visit friends and gamble," said Gordon Lam, a local restaurateur, "In the evening they usually walked to Prince Rupert along the railway tracks."

"In the 1960s there was a local train running between Port Edward and Prince Rupert in the evening," said Rudolf Jones, a retired CN conductor. "Many Chinese workers used to take that train to Prince Rupert to watch movies."

Gradually, fewer Chinese men and women worked in the fish canneries. Unlike the old-timers, the new immigrants and the Canadian-born Chinese had better chances of finding other employment. Many of them were quite young so they went back to school to study or to upgrade their skills at the community college, in order to get better jobs. Currently, three Chinese technicians now work in the Allied Pacific Processors, and a few other Chinese tradesmen work at the Aero Trading Company and the Ocean Fisheries Ltd. in Prince Rupert.

The Chinese Railroad Workers.

In British Columbia, the construction of the Grand Trunk Pacific Railway began at Prince Rupert and moved eastward to meet the extension from Alberta. The stretch of railway along the rocky bank of the Skeena River was the most difficult to construct and caused many deaths.[10] Consequently, the construction was behind schedule, and more labourers were needed to speed up the project. The Grand Trunk Pacific Company asked the Federal Government to relax the restrictions and allow the Company to employ Chinese labourers so that the railway could be completed on time. The request was turned down by the British Columbia Government which insisted that the GTP company honor the clause of "white labours only."[11] Thus, not many Chinese labourers were employed by the GTP other than as cooks in the railroad camps. Those Chinese labourers employed in construction, usually worked in high-risk areas where Caucasians refused to work.

By 1916, both the Grand Trunk Pacific and the Canadian Northern Railway were in serious financial difficulties, and in 1919, GTP went into receivership. The Federal Government appointed a Royal Commission, headed by J.M. Rosewear, to investigate the problems. The Report of the Commission recommended nationalization and amalgamation of the railways. Ultimately, the Government took over the two railways and called the new system the Transcontinental Canadian/National Railway Company (CN) in 1922.[12] Chinese immigrants were employed by CN only after WWII.

In the 1960s, when more Chinese immigrants arrived in Prince Rupert, Chinese young men hired on with the CN as yardmen and maintenance men. Gordon Lam's father was one of these CN employees. When Gordon arrived in Prince Rupert in 1966, he also worked for the CN for a short period of time before he set up his own restaurant business. Following the Second World War, young Canadian Chinese had access to post-secondary education. Some of these graduates joined the CN as engineers, technicians or tradesmen. At present, several Chinese Canadians are still working for the CN at Prince Rupert.

Chinese Employment in the Skeena Cellulose Corporation

Another industry that plays a vital role in sustaining the Prince Rupert economy, is the Skeena Cellulose Corporation. Its pulp mill is situated on Watson Island, south of the city. When this industry began in 1946, it was operated under the name of Columbia Cellulose Company, a subsidiary of the Celanese Corporation of America. In the beginning, the Columbia Celluose Company operated a dissolving sulphite pulp facility to produce raw materials for the production of cellulose acetate. In 1966, the Columbia Cellulose Company and the Skeena Cellulose of Sweden combined to form Skeena Kraft Limited which produced high quality kraft pulp for paper mills. Labour disputes and economic crises have caused this corporation continuing financial difficulties. When faced with environmental issues in 1976, the company shut down its sulphite operation permanently. After a number of changes in ownership, in 1986 this company became the Skeena Cellulose Corporation. In 1997 the BC Government, the TD Bank and the employees of the company took over the ownership of the corporation, which sells most of its products to Japan, China, South East Asia, United States and Europe.

Although the history of this industry is somewhat turbulent, the pulp mill has offered employment to many Canadians, including a number of Chinese Canadians and immigrants. Its establishment has also helped the development of Terrace, Carnaby and Smithers, as Skeena Cellulose has several sawmills in these areas to produce wood chips for its pulp mill and timber products for export. Since its inception, Skeena Cellulose has employed Chinese people as truck drivers, machine operators, wood-chips inspectors, and mechanics.

Other Chinese Occupations

Prince Rupert has two famous tailor shops on Third Avenue owned and operated by Chinese Canadians. They are the Lorne Tailor, established in the 1950s, and the Fashion Tailoring Shop, in 1964. Wong Horne is the owner of the Fashion Tailoring Shop.

"When I first arrived in 1959, Prince Rupert was a busy city," said Wong. "A good number of Chinese families had already arrived by then, but the Chinese population still consisted mainly of single men working in fish

A well known Chinese tailor shop in Prince Rupert.

Photo by Lily Chow

canneries in the vicinity of Prince Rupert. While many of these cannery workers came from Vancouver, over the years some of them settled here."

Wong and his cousin immigrated to Canada in 1955 under the sponsorship of their uncle. Soon after their arrival, his cousin went to Prince Rupert to work in the fish canneries. After a year or so, he left the cannery job to open a tailor shop. The tailoring business seems to be the family trade, for his father also operated a tailor shop in Vancouver. Wong worked in Vancouver for four or five years but did not see his future there. Ultimately, he went to Prince Rupert and joined his cousin in the tailoring business.

In 1964, he opened the Fashion Tailoring Shop and has operated the business ever since. Two years after he established the tailoring business, he took a trip to Hong Kong where he met Amy. They married and returned to Prince Rupert to continue with the tailoring business. They have two daughters, Kathy and Carol, who have been raised and educated in Prince Rupert.

Wong is well known for his involvement in the community. He is a key member of the Chinese Freemason Society and an active member of the Prince Rupert Chinese Association. In the late 1980s, he was elected as the president of the Prince Rupert Chinese Association. He is a long-standing member of the Kaien Island Lions Club and was awarded the Melvin Jones Fellowship by the Lions Club in 1994. As his children have all grown up, he could retire and enjoy his time, but he still continues with his trade.

"Sewing has become my hobby today. It does not make much money but it gives me a sense of self-satisfaction," commented Wong.

"In the 1960s many Chinese people owned and operated restaurants," Wong continued. "One of the earliest restaurants, the Grand Café, was owned by my wife's uncle and two other partners."

The Grand Café has left many fond memories in Prince Rupert. During World War II, the Grand Café gave credit to its clients and provided food to the poor and hungry who came to its doorstep. Rudolf Jones, a retired CN conductor, has pleasant memories of the Grand Café:

"The Grand Café was so busy in the early 1960s," said Jones. " I remember one of the fellows got excited easily. When the restaurant was crowded with customers, he would call out the orders with a loud and hoarse voice instead of writing it down on a piece of paper. The three partners Low Kut, Low Get Jing and Low Jack were very friendly people." Unfortunately, the Grand Café burned down in 1968.

The 1968 directory listed 11 Chinese restaurants in Prince Rupert, and one, the Paramount Café, in Port Edward. The names of the restaurants and their owners were listed in both English and Chinese characters in *The BC Interior*

Supplement phone directory produced by Chinese merchants in Vancouver. These restaurants offered jobs such as cooks, kitchen helpers and waiters or waitresses to Chinese immigrants. However, the immigrants usually worked in the restaurants owned and operated by relatives.

Josie Mah worked as a waitress in her father's restaurant when she first arrived from Hong Kong in 1951. In the following year she met her husband in Prince Rupert. She was the first Chinese bride to have a full-scale reception in the city. After her marriage, she worked in the Imperial Palace Restaurant, which was owned and operated by her husband.

When Josie first arrived in the city, she found life rather quiet and she felt isolated. There were few young Chinese girls of her age. In the 1950s she often encountered name-calling by the whites and natives, especially when they were drunk.

In the good old days when salmon runs were good and catches were abundant, people in Prince Rupert had money. Since the city had few recreational facilities in the 1950s, many men resorted to drinking. Some of these drunkards would lie on the streets snoring away, while others would shout and tease women as they passed by. Amy S. Wong, who arrived at Prince Rupert in 1965, has similar memories.

"Soon after I arrived in Prince Rupert, I worked in the Melrose Café," said Wong, the proprietor of the Fairview Restaurant. "I was scared to walk home alone after work in the evening because of the many drunkards lying in the streets. Very often I had to wait for my aunt to finish her day and walk me home."

Needless to say, such behavior was intimidating for young girls and women, particularly for those who could not speak English. One would never know how the drunkards would behave. As the city expanded its recreation facilities, fewer people consumed alcohol in excess. Gradually the sight of drunkards lying in the streets faded. As time went by, most of the Chinese women, who had immigrated to the city during the 1950s, acquired some English and could communicate with other Canadians. Now they not only found life pleasant and comfortable in the community, but also gained some understanding of other cultures.

In 1968, other Chinese businesses included Ted's Billiard Room, Star Confectionery Store, Kim's Produce, and one Shell service station and garage. Most of these businesses were set up on Second and Third Avenues. In 1997 a good number of Chinese restaurants were still in operation. Some of the older ones like the Chatay House, the Rex Café, the Hollywood Restaurant and the Commodore Restaurant were either sold or closed down, but new ones such as the Galaxy, the Fairview, the Green Apple, and the Stardust have been established in the last decade.

"There are so many Chinese restaurants in this city but very few fish and chips stores," said Gordon Lam. "I cannot see the reason for not making use of our own halibut. After all this city is known as the Halibut Capital of the World." The Green Apple Restaurant, owned and operated by Lam, does not serve conventional Canadian Chinese food but offers deep-fried halibut and chips.

In 1966, Lam immigrated to Canada with his mother, two sisters and two brothers. As he was still a teenager, he attended school in Prince Rupert before exploring the rest of the province.

"It was pretty tough for new immigrants to learn English when they first arrived," commented Lam. "I went to school at the beginning. But as a teenager I needed some pocket money. So after school I went to CN to wash coaches. On weekends I worked at Pagoda Inn peeling potatoes. It was not easy to juggle school and jobs. After a couple of years I left school and went to Vancouver to find my future."

But it did not work out for him. He returned to Prince Rupert and then attended cooking school in Terrace. Courses completed, he returned to Prince Rupert and opened a Chinese restaurant, the Happy Dragon, with two friends. After a year or so, his partners left the business and, with the help of his wife, Gordan decided to run the business himself.

"Restaurant business is time and energy consuming," Lam continued. "I have to get up very early to prepare food for the day. Competition is intense because there are so many Chinese restaurants in town. Soon after I acquired the Happy Dragon, my wife was expecting a baby and she could not help me very much. It was a juggling act to run a Chinese restaurant by myself. So I decided to change my business to a fish and chips joint which is less taxing."

Just like any conscientious parents, the Lams want the best for their children. They believe that a good education will help in preparing their children to face challenges in life. At the same time, they want their children to remember their roots. Thus, Gordon not only observes Chinese traditions at home but also participates in the cultural activities of the Chinese organizations. In 1997 he was elected as the President of the Prince Rupert Chinese Association and was actively involved in organizing and administrating the Chinese Heritage School.

Another civic-minded person is Danny Mah, the owner of Snappy Photo Center, a photo printing shop at 615 Third Avenue in Prince Rupert. While he was in China, Mah began school in his village at the age of four and continued his high school education in Guangzhou before he came to Canada. In 1951, Mah's father, who had been working for Edward Mah in the Sunrise Grocery Store, sponsored Danny to come to Canada. Sixteen years old, he attended Booth High School and picked up English in no time. The following year, Mah senior also sent for his wife and daughter.

"After three years in school I went to work," said Danny Mah. "I have been a truck driver delivering produce to restaurants and grocery shops. I worked as a meat cutter later on. In 1966, my cousins Ted, Henry and I opened the Imperial Palace Restaurant. A few years ago I left the restaurant business and started the photo printing shop."

Mah often volunteers in community work and supports numerous projects that benefit the community. He has been a member of the Prince Rupert Rotary Club for thirty years and has earned the Paul Harris Fellow Service Award for his perfect attendance. He is also a member of the Citizens on Patrol. In the Chinese community he is an active member of the Prince Rupert Chinese Association and an executive member of the Chinese Freemason Society. He has been elected president of the Chinese Association twice.

In addition, some Chinese Canadians in Prince Rupert have worked for the mining companies in the Stikine-Stewart region where silver, copper and other base metals are found. As many of these mines are located in remote areas, some mining companies provide bonuses to the workers as means of encouraging them to stay working. Previously, the companies offered free airline tickets to the workers to take holidays anywhere in BC after they had completed working four months with one of the companies. If the workers returned to the mines after their vacations, they would be welcomed with open arms and would be given another air ticket at the end of the next four months. No matter how good the bonuses were, though, most of the workers would leave when they could find work in urban areas.

Finding a Rainbow

Today, the Chinese Canadian population of the city is approximately 300, but this number has fluctuated with the economic and political conditions of the city. When Charles Hays announced his wonderful plan for the city, many Chinese immigrants migrated there. The fishing industry also kept Chinese people coming to the surrounding areas. However, during the Great Depression many Chinese immigrants moved away. When Prince Rupert became a military base for Canada and the United States in WW II, the wartime activities attracted other Chinese immigrants. The revision of the Immigration Act and the establishment of the Skeena Cellulose pulp mill also brought in large numbers of Chinese Canadians and Chinese immigrants, but in recent years the number of Chinese Canadians in the city started to diminish. A CN employee offered the following explanation:

"Remember, the old folks came here to look for a better life. Of course, the Lower mainland offers a more comfortable life; at least, the weather is milder there. Naturally when they retire, they move to warmer places to enjoy the fruits of their labour. Similarly, young people prefer to stay in the lower mainland after they complete their college or university education because they can get the jobs they want in larger cities. The traditional old folks like to stay with their children, and so they follow their children to the big cities. To keep the young people in town there must be jobs that give them the opportunities to move ahead in life here."

Many Chinese residents are optimistic as they can see the potential of this city developing small industries related to the fisheries as well as other resources. They did not lose their optimism during the 1997 economic crisis. For instance, at this time the dispute over the BC and Alaska fishing boundaries has lead to a blockade of the harbour, trapping many cruise ships at Prince Rupert. In retaliation, the Americans stopped using Prince Rupert as an Alaska cruise terminal, putting a damper on the tourism industry there. Adding to all of this, the future of Skeena Cellulose, a major employer in town, is uncertain.

"At present business may be slow," said Gordon Lam. "But the surrounding areas are endowed with many natural resources and mineral deposits. Once these areas are developed, the economy will pick up again."

"If the fishery industry could expand to include other seafood products, a substantial revenue can be secured, too," Lam continued. "People all over the world love to consume lobsters, crabs, oysters and prawns. If these crustaceans are cultivated, just like the salmon, they can provide a considerable income to the fishery industry. In addition, there is a potential market for jellyfish, sea cucumbers, octopus, squid and scallops in Asian countries as they are delicacies to many Asian people. Today, large quantities of these marine creatures in dehydrated form are exported from China and Japan, and are sold in Asia as well as in all the Chinatowns in North America. We can get into these fish markets easily since the surrounding water is full of these marine creatures. What we need now is someone with good capital to invest and develop these fishery resources."

These remarks certainly add hope and brighten the future for Prince Rupert. In Lam's view, politicians in all levels of Governments should listen and entrepreneurs should invest and develop plants for dehydrating marine life, as this industry could offer more employment and bring more revenue to the city, hence bringing the city one step closer to the pot of gold at the end of the rainbow.

This chapter has mentioned the existence of Chinese organizations in Prince Rupert but why they were formed and how they affected the lives of the Chinese residents has not been discussed. Chapter 5 addresses the role of these organizations.

Chapter 5

PRINCE RUPERT II

Chinese Beliefs and Values

Traditional Chinese teachings foster the practice of showing honor to teachers and their work, filial devotion to elders and parents, and recognition of kinship ties among people from the same village. A large number of Chinese Canadians firmly believe in these teachings, and they are not shy about expressing their values. As Danny Mah in Prince Rupert puts it, "I find it disappointing to see a young child addressing elders and teachers by their first names. It sounds rude and disrespectful. To me, that kind of greeting shows poor manners and is not acceptable in traditional Chinese society. Even at my age, I always greet my friends as Mr. or Mrs. so and so. I feel it is only right to address my superiors as sir or madam."

Showing filial devotion to elders and parents is demonstrated by the practice of sending money home to ensure that their parents and grandparents are living comfortably. In the past, the fact that many Chinese men accepted brides chosen by their parents illustrated their obedience and filial devotion. That many Chinese Canadians bring their grandparents and parents to Canada for family reunions indicates how much they care for and love their family and elders.

As the early Chinese immigrants came to Canada with the common goal of finding better lives for themselves as well as for their folks at home, many immigrants encouraged relatives and villagers to join them, once they found means of making a decent living. Mah Boon Kuan in Prince Rupert is a good example. Because he valued kinship, he helped many of his relatives to immigrate to Canada. When they arrived, he looked after them and provided jobs for them in the Sunrise Grocery store or in his railroad-tie making business. The new immigrants, in turn, would assist others from the same village to emigrate. Consequently, the Chinese community in Prince Rupert consists of many Chinese immigrants bearing the surname Mah or are related to the Mahs by marriage. This kind of chain migration was a common trend among the early Chinese immigrants to this country.

However, individual effort and assistance was not enough when large groups of immigrants from other counties in Guangdong arrived in a community. As early Chinese immigrants were usually absentee husbands, they needed the warmth and friendship of their countrymen to fill the void. To achieve that they usually lived in a communal house so that they could keep one another company, share each other's interests and concerns, and help one another maintain their ties to home by helping write letters or sending money home. The language barrier and cultural differences isolated them from other Canadians. Furthermore, many immigrants came to Prince Rupert when the anti-Chinese movement was strong and Chinese immigrants were treated as aliens. Thus the Chinese immigrants formed social organizations to protect themselves from prejudice and discrimination, to help them to find work and to represent them in the Canadian society when necessary. These organizations also gave the Chinese immigrants a sense of belonging, as they were able to use their own language and follow Chinese customs.

Chinese Organizations

In Prince Rupert there are three Chinese organizations: the Chinese Freemasons Society, the Chinese Nationalist League (Guomindang) and the Prince Rupert Chinese Association, each formed in a different time period. As well, there are two religious groups, the Prince Rupert Chinese Christian Fellowship and the Chinese Salvation Army. The Chinese Nationalist League was formed out of the patriotism of its members towards China. Its main objective was to support the revolutionary movement in China at the turn of the twentieth century to overthrow the imperial Qing Government.

The Chinese Nationalist League in Prince Rupert became dormant after World War II. The Chinese Freemasons Society and the Prince Rupert Chinese Association are still very active and participate in many multicultural events.

The Chinese Freemasons Society

The earliest Chinese organization in Prince Rupert was a chapter of the Chinese Freemasons (Hongmen Minzhidang) in Canada. The Chinese

Freemasons Societys' history dates back to the beginning of the Qing Dynasty. After the Manchus occupied China in 1644, a revolutionary body known as Hongmen Hui was formed with the objective of overthrowing the Qing Dynasty and restoring the Ming Dynasty. To the Ming loyalists, it was a disgrace and humiliation to be governed by the Manchus whom they considered as aliens.

Members of the Hongmen Hui often carried out subversive activities to attack the Qing Government but the Qing soldiers crushed their insurrections. During the Taiping Peasant Movement, which began in 1850, the Hongmen Hui became a strongforce. When the Taiping Movement failed, members of the Hongmen Hui were persecuted and forced into exile. Many of them escaped to North America and South East Asia and set up chapters in these countries, hoping that they would be able to return to China one day to overthrow the Qing dynasty. This did not happen.

When Dr. Sun Yet Sen came to North America to promote his revolutionary democratic principles and lobby for help from the overseas Chinese to carry out his mission, he became a member of the Chinese Freemasons Society. The Chinese Freemasons Society was willing to help and mortgaged their properties in Victoria and in Toronto to help Sun in the revolution. At the same time, Sun also helped the Chinese Freemasons Society to amend its constitution. Thus the name of the society was changed from Zhigongtang to Minzhidang, meaning a political party governed or controlled by the people.

After the formation of the Chinese Republic in 1911, Sun turned his back on the Chinese Freemasons Society. According to senior members, Sun had planned to assimilate the Chinese Freemasons Society into his party, the Guomindang, thus creating a rift. To avoid dealing with or being controlled by the Guomindang, the Chinese Freemasons Society created the Dart Koon Club whose membership excluded any Guomindang supporters. Hence, Sun could not exercise any authority over the constitution and management of the club. The Dart Koon Club focused on training its members in martial arts for self-defence as well as teaching its members the lion and dragon dances.

Since then, the Chinese Freemasons have become a benevolent and cultural organization, especially in Canada, taking care of the aged and looking after the welfare of its members. It has provided financial assistance to members in need as well as offering hostel accommodations for visitors. Of course, members had to pay dues but they could borrow money from the organization to start small businesses or to help out when they were out of work. Among the social and cultural activities the Freemasons sponsored were publishing of newspapers, sponsoring of youth programs and providing recreation such as gambling and opium-smoking during the era of the Gold Rushes.[1]

The date the Chinese Freemasons Lodge was established in Prince Rupert cannot be ascertained. The *1983 Chinese Freemasons Anniversary Gazette*, published in Vancouver, stated that the chapter in Prince Rupert was established between 1882 to 1885 but there is no substantiating evidence. The Lodge in Prince Rupert could not have been erected earlier than the incorporation of the city in 1910 because there were not enough Chinese residents in the area at that time. As many of the Chinese workers in the fish canneries were members of the Chinese Freemasons Society, the 1882/85 claim may simply reflect the presence of Freemasons on the north coast. A Prince Rupert City Hall official speculated that the lodge building was erected somewhere between 1910 and 1920.[2] Old-timers think that the lodge was built around 1917.

Although this Chinese organization has existed in Prince Rupert longer than any other Chinese organizations, very little of its past activities was recorded. Many of the elders have left town or passed away. Present Chinese residents mention that they have heard that the Chinese cannery workers from Port Edward visited the Freemasons Lodge in the 1930s, where they read newspapers, socialized with friends and gambled. There is one piece of evidence which indicates that the society had been involved with the Chinese National Revolution. A group of Chinese Freemasons, who visited China in the 1980s, stated that the name of the Prince Rupert Chinese Freemasons Society is engraved in the monument at Huanghua Gang in Guangdong. During the 1911 Huanghua insurrection, 69 out of the 72 casualties were the members of the Chinese Freemasons. The Huaghua Gang monument was erected to recognize all the overseas Chinese organizations who contributed, in kind or money, to the Chinese Revolution.

The Prince Rupert Chinese Freemasons building was located at 815 Third Avenue. On June 24, 1971 the building was destroyed by fire resulting in the loss of all records and documents. At the time of the fire three members, Chong Hee Mah, Mah Gee Ow and Mah Lin were sleeping in the lodge. They escaped without injury but lost all their personal belongings. No one knew for sure how the fire was started except that it began at the back of the building. Some people speculated that an overheated wood stove might have been the cause. The total loss in the fire was estimated at about $60,000, but the Chinese Freemasons Society recovered about $28,000 from the insurance company, said Wong Horne.

After the fire, three members from the headquarters in Toronto came to

The fire which destroyed the Chinese Freemasons Building in 1971 resulted in the loss of much of Prince Rupert's Chinese history.

Prince Rupert Museum & Archives

Prince Rupert and suggested that the Lodge be closed. Zhou Bing Kun, Robert Zhang and the four other members of the Prince Rupert Chinese Freemasons Society disagreed, wanting to rebuild the Lodge. The visitors left without offering any help. Zhou asked the headquarters in Vancouver for assistance but the headquarters could not help the chapter unless the existing six members could recruit another twenty-five people to join the chapter. Zhou then invited Wong Horne to join the Society and asked him to help in a membership drive.

"It was not right to close down the chapter," said Jerry Jang. "It was a place where the Chinese old-timers could get together and socialize."

According to Wong and Jang, the Chinese Freemasons lodge provided accommodation to single men. During the era of the contract system in fish canneries, seasonal workers usually stayed in the lodge when they visited Prince Rupert.

After the meeting, Wong spearheaded the membership drive and the group eventually recruited thirty new members. Zhou and Wong then approached the headquarters in Vancouver again. Unfortunately, the headquarters had already promised to help another chapter at Port Moody and had no funds available. Ultimately, Zhou, Wong and three other key members went to a bank to get a mortgage of $60,000 under the name of Prince Rupert Chinese Freemasons Holding Company. A year later the Chinese Freemasons Lodge was reconstructed at 816-817, Third Avenue, West. The total cost for the new lodge was $89,000. In order to meet the mortgage payment, the ground floor of the building at 816 was rented to a laundry shop, and still is to this day. The building at 817 is now shared with the Prince Rupert Chinese Association, and is a meeting place for both organizations and many of their functions are held there.

Perhaps it was a blessing in disguise that the 1971 fire occurred, for after the fire the Freemasons Society revived its spirit like a phoenix arising from its ashes. In the last few decades, the Chinese Freemasons Society has carried out many cultural and social functions together with the Prince Rupert Chinese Association. Both organizations usually participate in the two important Chinese feast days, Qing Ming and Cong Yang. On these feast days, members go to the cemetery and place flowers, burn incense and offer sacrifices such as steamed fowl, pork, steamed rice, pastries and fruits at Chinese tombs.

This organization also joined the Prince Rupert Chinese Association in celebrating the Chinese New Year and has participated in other multicultural events. Although some of the founding members such as Robert Zhang and Zhou Bing Kun no longer live in town, the society remains active and its membership has increased to include a women's group. With the addition of new blood such as Allan Chan, Gordon Lam, Danny Mah, Zhou You and others, the society continues to grow. Chan has been a member of the Chinese Freemasons since he arrived in town and was elected as the president of the society in 1996. Wong Horne has served as president of the society four times since the rebuilding of the lodge. At present Wong is the president of the Dart Koon Club.

The Chinese Nationalist League

Chinese immigrants often dreamed of returning home one day after they had earned enough money to provide a better life for their families; therefore, they always paid close attention to the political activities and the transgressions of foreign powers in China. Near the end of the Qing Dynasty there was a nationalism movement in China initiated by Tongmen Hui, a revolutionary party formed by three prominent groups: the Zhongxing Hui led by Sun Yet Sen; the Huaxing Hui by Huang Xing; and Guangfu Hui by Cai Yuanpei. On October 10, 1911, the uprising at Wuchang succeeded in overthrowing the

Qing Government and the Republic of China was formed with Tongmeng Hui as the governing party. The Tongmen Hui later changed its name to Guomindang or the Chinese Nationalist League.

The Guomindang Government was not in control of all of China. The northern part of China was under the control of Yuan Shikai, a powerful general of the Qing regime. The last Emperor, Pu Yi, was still sitting on the throne in Beijing. Dr. Sun Yet Sen had to negotiate with Yuan to remove Pu Yi. When Yuan succeeded, he became the first President of the Republic. Yuan was a self-serving person who wanted to dissolve parliament and become the emperor. His biggest blunder was signing the humiliating Twenty-one Demands Treaty with Japan, giving Japan the rights to occupy Shandong province and to exploit the mineral wealth in southern Manchuria. These issues triggered the second revolution in China aimed at overthrowing the Yuan Government. Foreign aid was very much needed to support Dr. Sun Yet Sen's fight against Yuan. By then a number of Guomindang branches had already formed in Canada. On February 16, 1919 the *Prince Rupert Daily News* reported fifty-six branches of the Guomindang were in Canada. At that time friction between the Guomindang and the Chinese Freemasons resulted in the Chinese Freemasons losing interest in the Republican Government. The Guomindang branches became agents to collect funds from overseas Chinese to support the Republican Government. Also, the overseas Guomindang were responsible for informing the overseas Chinese in North America about the situation in China and for preaching the Three People's Principles of the Guomindang party–People's Nationalism, People's Democracy and People's Livelihood–to its members.

In Prince Rupert, the Guomindang branch was located at 836, Third Avenue. One record book of the Chinese Salvation Bureau (Jiu Guo Hui) indicates the role of the Guomindang branch prior to WWII. In 1931 when Japan invaded Manchuria, a Chinese territory in the northeast, all the branches of Guomindang in Canada formed a subcommittee, the Chinese Salvation Bureau, whose main objective was to help the Republican Government to resist the Japanese invasion. The record book states that a meeting was held on February 4, 1931, in which one hundred and twenty members attended. During the meeting Leong Bao Chang was elected as president, Huang Ping as secretary and Liu Ying Zhi as treasurer with eight other members on the committee. Everyone present donated from $1 to $35 to the war effort against the Japanese. A total of $571.28 was collected. After some discussion, it was decided to send the money to the Nineteenth Chinese Army Corps through the Republican Government in Nanking (Nanjing).

During World War II, the Guomindang in Canada was actively involved in raising funds to support the Chinese Republic in resisting the Japanese aggression. According to old-timers, the Guomindang branch in Prince Rupert demanded its members to donate a certain portion of their wages towards the war effort. One member who refused to donate the required sum was physically assaulted by an executive officer. The Guomindang branch also raised funds for the war effort through bake sales and selling artificial flowers and small Chinese flags to the public.

In 1948 the Communist Party took over China and declared the country the People's Republic. Since then many influential Chinese merchants left the Guomindang branches in Canada, leaving core members to manage the headquarters in large cities and to keep in contact with Taiwan where the Guomindang Government was exiled. The Guomindang branches in smaller cities became less active and eventually disappeared. As time went by the Guomindang in Prince Rupert became dormant but the rooms in its building were rented out to single men and new immigrants who could not find immediate accommodations. In 1966, Gordon Lam and his brothers stayed there for a short period when they first arrived in Prince Rupert.

"When we first arrived, my parents and two sisters were staying with our grandfather," said Lam. "The house of my grand father was too small to accommodate all of us. My parents rented out a room in the Chinese Nationalist League building at 836 W. Third Avenue for me and my brother to live there temporarily. The living conditions there are hard to forget. There was no central heating system; the whole building was kept warm by the kitchen wood stove, which was also used for boiling water and for cooking simple meals. At night, especially in winter, we stuffed the stove with wood before we went to bed. Then we left our bedroom door ajar so that warm air could circulate. In midwinter when the temperature plunged down after the fire went out, it was quite a challenge to get up in the morning."

In 1975 there were only five single men living in the Guomindang Building. As there was no revenue apart from the meagre rental income, the property tax had not been paid for three years. At one time there had been an offer to purchase the building for $25,000. Wong Horne, who was the president of the Prince Rupert Chinese Association at that time, felt that it was not right to sell the building, because early Chinese immigrants had donated money to build it. He believed that the building should be kept as a heritage property. As the Prince Rupert Chinese Association did not have a building, Wong suggested the Association negotiate with the Guomindang headquarters to take over the building and pay the headquarters a minimal sum. Some members of the

Chinese Association were against the idea because it would cost a large sum of money to renovate the building. Wong called a general meeting to discuss his proposal.

The membership voted that unless they could find enough money for the project, they would not support the proposal. After the meeting one member, who preferred to remain anonymous, donated $25,000 for the renovation project and other expenses such as the transfer of ownership and the payment of property taxes. In the meantime Wong and Earl Mah approached the BC Government for assistance. Iona Campagnola, the MLA, managed to obtain a loan of $10,000 for them. Unfortunately, the building burned down on June 23, 1978 before they could proceed with renovations. That fire also destroyed all the documents and artifacts except records of the Chinese Salvation Bureau. The $10,000 assistance was returned to the Government but the Chinese Association kept the $25,000 donation from the anonymous member. Hence the existence of the Guomindang in Prince Rupert has become a distant memory.

The Prince Rupert Chinese Association

Prior to 1948, the Chinese Nationalist League was looked upon as a paternalistic body that would represent the Chinese immigrants and provide them with guidance and protection in the community. With its decline after the Communist victory in China, the Chinese immigrants lost their direction. Many of the Chinese immigrants, including the new arrivals, had some reservations about joining the existing Chinese Freemasons Society because of its secretive nature and past subversive activities.

"Many of the Chinese Canadians assumed that the Chinese Freemasons Society was some sort of a gang or underground organization and they did not want to join the organization for fear of getting into trouble," said Francis Wong. "It was a misunderstanding. Nowadays, the Chinese Freemasons Society is a registered benevolent association."

The Chinese Freemasons Society had performed some good deeds for the Chinese immigrants in the past, despite its faults and failings. However, it is understandable why some Chinese Canadians in the last few decades preferred not to join the Chinese Freemasons Society, especially the Chinese immigrants. They did not want to get involved with an organization that appeared in any way suspicious. They wanted to become law-abiding citizens and did not want to suffer from any prejudice. Moreover, they were not sojourners and Canada would be their home. They wanted to live peacefully here, but understood that some sort of organization was needed.

In the 1950s, prejudice and discrimination against the Chinese Canadians was still present. At that time most of the new Chinese immigrants could not get the job they applied for even though they could speak English. A good number of them worked for other Canadians but were not paid the promised wages. Without a representing body to help and speak for them, they felt lost and helpless. Besides, an apolitical and benevolent association would certainly help to bridge the gaps between the Chinese residents and other Canadians in the community.

"When I first arrived in Prince Rupert I could sense the subtle discriminations," said Danny Mah. "Many jobs in the public sector were not available to the Chinese Canadians and immigrants. At times, Chinese Canadians ventured to apply for jobs that were advertised. Nine times out of ten they could not get the positions. Consequently, they gave up applying for jobs elsewhere but stayed on working for their own families in small businesses."

In 1953, the late Li Jue Min, a well-known Chinese merchant from southern BC who visited Prince Rupert frequently, encouraged the Chinese residents in Prince Rupert to form a Chinese Association. He hosted a Chinese New Year Dinner for all Chinese residents and spoke to them about the importance of having an association that could speak for them as well as inform them about the political and economic development of their adopted country. He said such an organization should attempt to provide help and protection for the Chinese residents, to maintain open dialogue with its members and to promote friendship among its members. He also stressed that such an organization should take the initiative to reach out and share Chinese culture with other Canadians as a means of promoting better understanding of the Chinese people and their culture.

Immediately after the dinner, an interim committee was formed to draft out the constitution and a date was set for the first election of officers. On April 31, 1953, executive members and board of directors were elected. They christened the organization the Prince Rupert Chinese Association. Since its inception, the Prince Rupert Chinese Association has been very active and has made every attempt to look after the welfare of the Chinese residents and to reach out to other Canadians in the community.

An incident in 1960 had proved the necessity and the strength of the Prince Rupert Chinese Association. In June 1960, the RCMP went to the Chinese community and demanded that every Chinese resident show his or her proof of immigration and asked the Chinese Association to give them its membership list. The RCMP officers claimed that the campaign of obtaining information on all Chinese residents was an order from the Immigration Department in Ottawa. It was to find out if there were any illegal Chinese immigrants in the city. The Chinese Association called an emergency meeting to deal with the issue. All felt that the RCMP action was an infringement on privacy, especially as there was no evidence of illegal activities.

One of the executive members phoned the Chinese Benevolent Association in Vancouver for guidance. Foon Sien, a past president of the Chinese Benevolent Association, felt that such an investigation directed against an entire group of people of one racial origin was an act of intimidation and racism. He advised them to reject the RCMP demands. The Prince Rupert Chinese Association also hired A. B. Brown, a lawyer in Prince Rupert, to deal with the issue on its behalf. In the meantime the 200 Chinese residents stood firm and refused to co-operate with the RCMP. Later, C.W. Harvison, the RCMP commissioner denied that such order had been made.[3] Finally the matter came to a close with no further requests from the RCMP.

In the last three decades or so, discrimination in Prince Rupert has become less prevalent. Recently the Chinese residents have adopted an tolerant attitude towards racism. They recognize that racism hurts but retaliation does not solve the problem.

"When an unpleasant incident takes place we have to see if it hurts our dignity or causes discord in the community. If it does not hurt, the best thing is to ignore it," remarked Gordon Lam. "At times people say things without realizing their remarks could hurt the feelings of others. In such instances it is our responsibility to point out his or her ignorance politely, instead of making an issue out of it."

"Occasionally we get some teasing about Chinese manners or ways of behaving," added Amy S. Wong. "It really depends on who makes these remarks and how they are made. If such comments come from an acquaintance with no intention to hurt or discriminate, I will ignore it, too. It is foolish to create tension in a small community where most of the people are friendly and nice."

Besides dealing with external issues, the Prince Rupert Chinese Association also assisted Chinese members in the community in resolving internal conflicts on a few occasions as well as providing interpretation services and legal aid to those who had difficulties in obtaining counsel. When old-timers without family members close by passed away, the Chinese Association took the responsibility of looking after the burials, tracing their families in China and sending the estates, if any, back to their families. In addition, the Association purchased some plots in the cemetery in advance so that whenever a member in the Chinese community passed away, he or she could be buried near other Chinese.

"This is to make it easier for us to hold our ritual in Qing Ming and Cong Yang when we go to the cemetery to pay respects during those festivals. We can do everything in one area instead of going over the whole cemetery to look for Chinese markers," said Gordon Lam.

At one time the executive members and board of directors contemplated constructing a building for the Chinese Association. They could not do so because of the heavy expenses. As mentioned, they attempted to take over the Guomindang building but it was destroyed by fire in 1978. Now, the Chinese Association shares the premises of the Chinese Freemasons Society at 817, Third Avenue.

Throughout its forty-odd years of history, the Chinese Association has participated in many multicultural events and carried out charity work in the community. Among other events, the Chinese Association has participated in the celebrations of the BC Centennial in 1958, the fiftieth Anniversary of Prince Rupert in 1960, and the Canadian Centennial in 1967. On these occasions and many since, its members and the members of the Chinese Freemasons performed the lion dance, and young girls carrying lanterns joined in the parade. Recently, a beautiful float resembling a Chinese palace has been added.

When the new parade began, the Chinese community was awarded first prize because the dazzling costumes worn by participants and the colorful decorations on the float were outstanding. The Chinese Association has also participated in Folkfest and Seafest many times. During Seafest the Chinese restaurants sold food and the revenues from the sales were donated to the Association for operating expenses. A great portion of the money was set aside for the Chinese Heritage School and for scholarship funds.

Whenever possible the Chinese Association also helped with charity work in the community. In the early 1960s, members of the Association canvassed on behalf of the hospital to purchase an X-ray mobile unit. It also donated money to charity organizations such as the Salvation Army, the United Way and others. It offered scholarships for the top graduates in the public schools, as well as for the best Chinese students no matter what their grade level. In 1997 the recipients of the Prince Rupert Chinese Association scholarships were Mark Seidel and Bernice Liu, each receiving $400. They were the top graduates in Charles Hays Secondary School and Prince Rupert Secondary School respectively. The scholarship was conditional on enrollment in a post-secondary institution. In addition, Bernice Liu and Hugh Leong were given another $100 scholarship for being the top Chinese students in the city.

The recipient of the top Chinese student scholarship must be a member of the Prince Rupert Chinese Association as well. The funds for these scholarships came from the interest on the Chinese Association's long-term deposits in a bank, food sale proceeds during Seafest, tickets sold during Chinese New Year and the profits from the sale of raffle tickets. In 1997 the first prize from the raffle tickets was $400, second prize $200 and third prize $100. The money left over was used for future scholarships and as a donation to the hospital.

The Chinese Association has been conscientious in promoting and perpetuating Chinese culture. Members recognize that Chinese culture has many facets. Besides authentic Chinese food, culture also includes language, literature, and arts such as painting, calligraphy, music, and dance. It also includes the celebration of the various festivals. From the very beginning, the Chinese Association attempted to establish a Chinese school and organize Chinese folk dance sessions for young children. At one time the Chinese Association invited Wong Hey Yin (Huang Xiran), a professional dance instructor of the Huang Dance Academy in Vancouver, to give a series of workshops and to teach 16 young girls to perform the ribbon dance (Dun Huang Wu), the fan dance and the lantern dance. These dances were performed in the Folkfest of 1988 and received high praise. When Tim Mah, a gentleman who had some training in martial arts, was in town he and Danny Mah taught the young boys Chinese martial arts.

Since the Chinese New Year is the most important Chinese festival, the Association celebrates Chinese New Year almost every year. During the festival season more than 100 Chinese residents are involved in the preparation. They usually hold the celebration at the Elks Hall and invite the city dignitaries and local MLAs to join them. The money collected from ticket sales is donated to the scholarship fund. The celebration usually begins with a traditional lion dance in step with the beating of drums and clashing of cymbals. Then the president of the Chinese Association greet the dignitaries, guests and others in the audience. He wishes everyone *gongxi facai*, meaning "have a prosperous New Year." Normally the dignitaries address the audience and offer their best wishes and New Year's greetings to the members of the Chinese community. After all of the speeches have been made, the guests and audience are invited to a buffet dinner that includes traditional Chinese dishes and seafood. Martial arts demonstrations, Chinese folk dances, music and songs entertain the audience. Sometimes the entertainment includes men and women modeling Chinese costumes, which they have borrowed from Zheng Hua Xing, a Chinese organization in Vancouver. Towards the end of the celebration, prizes and gifts donated by local merchants are presented to lucky ticket-holders.

The Chinese Heritage School

The first endeavor of the Prince Rupert Chinese Association was to establish a Chinese School. To the Chinese residents it was important to foster the Chinese language and culture in the younger generations. In 1954 the Chinese Association established the Prince Rupert Chinese School. The teaching staff consisted of eight young adults, mostly mothers, who took turns giving instructions from 4-6 pm Monday to Friday. There were about 25 students, including both Canadian-born children and Chinese immigrant children. Classes were held in the Guomindang building at 836 Third Avenue and the Guomindang Consulate in Vancouver supplied the textbooks. When the Guomindang Consulate was dismissed after the United Nations recognized the People's Republic of China, the school bought its own texts. School expenses were subsidized by the Chinese Association and came from donations by Chinese members in the community as well as fund raising activities such as film shows and bake sales.

"At the beginning we had three levels in the school, beginners, intermediate and advanced classes. Our curriculum included language arts, social studies, music and painting," said Danny Mah, one of the teachers. "The medium of instruction was Cantonese, but we taught our students to sing the Chinese National Anthem in Mandarin."

"Unfortunately this Chinese school could only operate for a couple years," Mah continued. "Students dropped out because they had to participate in extracurricular activities in their regular schools. The older ones wanted to earn some money and took on part-time jobs. Some teachers left town and others stopped teaching because they lost interest in teaching as the students dropped out."

As time went by, many Chinese residents were dismayed to find that their children could not speak Chinese well and often used English in their conversations at home and in the community. Also, some of the youngsters were so well integrated into the mainstream that they began to lose the traditional Chinese manners. In Chinese culture people do not address one another by their first names. Chinese children are taught at home to address the older ones of their own generations as brother or sister with their first names attached to their ranks like "Brother Chung" or "Sister Ying". They are supposed to address people of their parents' generation as uncle and aunt, and the elderly as grandpa or grandma.

In the 1970s Danny Mah reopened the Chinese School and taught classes with Mak Chow and other teachers, including one from China. They followed the same schedule as before and held their classes in the Guomindang building and later in the basement of the Chinese Freemasons building. Again, the school lasted only two years. The Chinese Christian Fellowship also attempted to revive the Chinese School twice, once in 1983 and then in 1993 with Rev. Andrea Tang as principal. The school was closed down after Tang left.

Though the operation of the Chinese school had failed in the past, the Chinese Association never gave up. In 1997 the executive members and other enthusiastic people established the Chinese Heritage School again. To them it is not only important for Chinese Canadian children to learn the language but also for them to retain Chinese customs.

"In Chinese culture, the younger generations are expected to look after their parents and grandparents when they grow old. Our Chinese Canadian children are not aware of this unless they are told," said Amy S. Wong, the principal of the school. "Although the seniors in Canada are more or less supported by the social system, they still need love and care, honor and respect. It is our hope that through the school we are able to impart some of the Chinese values such as filial devotion to parents and recognition of brotherhood to our children."

A couple of months of preparations were needed before classes began in the fall of 1997. First, they formed a school board of which Gordon Lam was the chairman, Michelle Lai the secretary, Amy S. Wong the principal, Guan Nan Hen the vice-principal, two instructional directors, one administrator and five teachers. Rev Lin Chih-Jung (Lin Zhirong) was the consultant. In that year about 48 students enrolled and attended the school, held every Saturday from 2:00-4:00 pm at the Prince Rupert campus of Northwest College. No fee was required but each student had to pay $10.00 per month to cover the cost of textbooks and other supplies. The textbooks were bought from San Lain Bookstore in Vancouver, while the teachers developed most of the exercises and other resources.

"So far, the attendance has been good. The parents are very supportive and have been encouraging their children to come to school," said Michelle Lai, a Chinese Canadian who immigrated from Malaysia.

The Chinese Religious Groups

When the early Chinese immigrants entered Canada, many registered themselves as Buddhist or Confucian. In the last few decades many Chinese Canadians have embraced the Christian faith and Chinese Christian churches have been established in many cities. Nowadays, two Chinese Christian groups are found in Prince Rupert: the Prince Rupert Chinese Christian Fellowship and the Chinese Salvation Army. A number of Chinese Canadians joined the Salvation Army as early as the mid-1950s. One of them was Colonel Check Yee who came from Hong Kong in 1951.

Colonel Yee, a journalist in Guangdong, China, was blacklisted by the Communist Government in 1949, and was forced into exile. In Hong Kong he married Phyllis Mah, a sister of Earl Mah, who was born in Prince Rupert. Soon the couple immigrated to Prince Rupert and Yee got a job delivering bread for the Prince Rupert Bakery owned by Earl Mah. He worked in the bakery for six years and then joined the Salvation Army. In 1957 he and his family moved to San Francisco where he became the pastor of the Salvation Army in Chinatown. After he retired from his pastoral career in 1994, he traveled around the world spreading the word of God. Today, some Chinese Canadians are still actively involved with the work of the Salvation Army in Prince Rupert.

The Prince Rupert Chinese Christian Fellowship began in 1960. This group has never belonged to any denomination, but is under the leadership and guidance of Francis Wong and his wife Marina Kan, a lawyer in town. The Fellowship receives subsidies and other forms of assistance such as Sunday sermon videotapes, newsletters and other Christian-faith-related materials from the Christ Church of China in Vancouver. The Prince Rupert Fellowship Baptist Church has been consistent in helping the Fellowship throughout the years, primarily by allowing it to use the Church premises for Sunday services and other faith-related activities.

Between 1960 and 1978 Pastor Lloyd Jackson of the Prince Rupert Fellowship Baptist Church was actively reaching out to the Chinese community, teaching new Chinese immigrants English and enrolling their children in the Sunday School of the church. In the summer of 1978, Allan Liu, a theology student, went to Prince Rupert from Vancouver and started Bible study sessions and Sunday worship with a group of Chinese residents. Since then theology students have gone to Prince Rupert to carry out pastoral ministry during the summer months. These ministers included Gentle Lee, Joseph Sun, Stephen Kwong, Andrea Tang, George Siu and Lin Chih-Jung (Lin Zhirong). Some of them also helped to carry out numerous Christian educational tasks such as the publication of their annual magazine "*Outreach*" in 1980, the reestablishment of a Chinese School in 1982 and in 1993, and the publication of "*Rainbow*" a monthly Chinese newsletter in 1997.

This Chinese Christian Fellowship was incorporated as a society in 1984. Since then Chinese Christian groups from Vancouver have visited Prince Rupert during summer to preach the Gospel. This Fellowship group holds its Sunday service at 2:00 pm at the Fellowship Baptist Church and weekly Bible study in the home of Francis Wong and Marina Kan. This Fellowship group also carries out visitations and outreach tasks in the Chinese community. Throughout the year the group holds various functions such as picnics, Christmas parties and other activities related to the Christian faith.

Although there have been two Chinese organizations and two religious groups in Prince Rupert for some time, many Chinese residents belong to more than one association. For example, Wong Horne belongs to both the Chinese Freemasons Society and the Prince Rupert Chinese Association. He was the president of the Chinese Association in 1957 and the president of the Chinese Freemasons in 1975, 1984, and 1995. Similarly, Francis Wong was the vice president of the Chinese Association in 1997 and also carried out pastoral work for the Chinese Christian Fellowship for many years.

In the early days the Chinese Freemasons Society attempted to assist, protect and provide recreation for its members who were mostly single men. The activities of the Chinese Nationalist League illustrated the concerns and sentiments of the early immigrants towards China. The Prince Rupert Chinese Association was formed out of the needs of the Chinese residents, especially those who could not communicate well with other Canadians when they immigrated to join family already in Prince Rupert. Their desires to find an organization to represent them in the community and to preserve Chinese culture and heritage also prompted the establishment of the association.

The religious groups attempted to preach the Gospel and evangelize those Chinese who did not have any religious faith. In short, there are at least four or five Chinese organizations in Prince Rupert but their mandates are relatively similar. They were formed with the general intention of giving support and assistance to one another, preserving traditions and cultures, fostering love and care, and strengthening their bonds of friendship.

Chapter Six

TERRACE

A Stopping Place.

Terrace, which is a trade and Government service center in the northwest region of British Columbia, is built on a series of steppes of the Coast Mountain Range at the confluence of the Skeena River and its tributary, the Kitsumkalum River. The mountains provide invaluable timber to forest industries such as logging and sawmills. Settlement in the area took place in the early 1900s when some of the early pioneers such as George Little, Henry Frank, Charles Weeks and others arrived there. At that time the Skeena River was a busy waterway with sternwheelers puffing from Port Essington to Hazelton, taking miners and provisions to the Interior. Large numbers of natives traveled on the Skeena River to work in the many fish canneries at Port Essington and along the Pacific coast during the fishing season. After the fishing season these natives went home via the Skeena River thus making the river a busy waterway prior to the completion of the Grand Trunk Pacific Railway (GTP) in 1914.

"When our family arrived in 1908, there was no city, only a store near the riverbank and a hotel nearby owned by George Little," said Floyd Frank, a well-known dairy farmer in Terrace. At the age of four he came up with his parents from Port Essington. In 1910, a school was established, which the Frank children attended.

"The land in this area was cheap," Frank continued. "It was sold at one dollar per acre. Many early pioneers bought acres of land and built their cabins there. In summer they went north to prospect and mine gold. In winter they hunted and trapped animals in the bush. In short, this was just a stopping place."

The Early Chinese

The presence of Chinese immigrants was noted in Terrace as early as 1916. A few of them worked as labourers in the construction of the GTP, in logging companies or sawmills, but most were cooks in railroad and logging camps, in mess halls of saw mills and in private homes. Also, two laundry men and a couple of Chinese farmers were making their living in Terrace around the same period of time.

The Chinese cooks

George Little, the founder of Terrace, had a Chinese cook called Sam in his sawmill. Sam worked in the sawmill for some time and then was 'promoted' to the Little's home as the family cook. After George Little sold his sawmill to Dudley Little, Chris Haugland and Duncan Kerr (LH& K) the sawmill was expanded to include several mess halls. In one of the mess halls was Moon, another Chinese cook. The word 'Moon' actually has a Chinese character, which means full (满).

"Moon was our favourite cook," said Mamie Kerby, the daughter of Chris Haugland, a director of the Heritage Park Museum in Terrace. "He was very hard working and always kept his kitchen meticulously clean and proper. Every morning he got up at the crack of dawn and wiped the floor of the mess hall before he prepared breakfast for the crew. He cooked all the meals without any help. In his spare time he went into the meat business. He bought a big chunk of meat, usually the best part, from a butcher shop nearby for retailing. He kept the meat on a tray covered with a screen casing in his kitchen. My mother often bought meat from him because she would always get what she wanted."

According to Kerby, Moon was very fond of children. The Haugland children loved to visit him. Every time they visited him, the boys would get a pie and the girls would be given butterfly cup cakes.

"This is how Moon made the butterfly cup cakes," Kerby recalled. "First, he cut off the top portion of the cup cake and filled the cut surface with jam. Then he sliced the top portion into half and placed them on the surface of the jam in such a way that they appeared like the wings of a butterfly"

Although Moon was working on two jobs most of the time, he still found time to gamble. He frequented two small gambling dens operated by L.K. Joe and Wing Hin. After working a few years for the LH& K, Moon left Terrace and went to Smithers to work as a cook in a hotel.

Dick Adams, a well-known business entrepreneur in Terrace, also had a favourite Chinese cook working in his gold mine, the Lucky Luke Gold Mine, near Usk, BC.

"My father was very fond of Lee Tong," said Helene McRae, the daughter of Dick Adams. " Lee became our friend. Once he came back from China and gave us a piece of beautiful silk. We had made blouses out of it. He used to give us lily bulbs to grow indoors at Christmas. He also gave us a set of mahjong tiles."

At Lakelse Lake a number of Chinese cooks worked in the logging camps. One Chinese man nicknamed "Hop-along" was a nervous person and he usually paced up and down when he became excited. Nothing much was noted about him except that he was a friendly person and got along well with people in the surrounding camps.

Unlike other nationalities, these Chinese cooks did not have to erect their own houses but lived in cabins or rooms provided by the companies if they were working in sawmills or logging camps. They lived alone or with other cooks in the same company, as their families had usually been left in China. Private cooks usually lived in cabins near the homes of their employers.

The Chinese laundry men

L. K. Joe and Wing Hin were the two laundry men in Terrace. Many Caucasian seniors still remember them for their services they provided while they were in Terrace.

"When we were kids we did not know the names of the two Chinese laundry men," said Mamie Kerby. "We just called them Little Joe and Long Tom."

Kerby described L. K. Joe, or Little Joe, as a small person about five feet tall. He always wore a well-starched white jacket and a pair of black pants. He had his business in a two-storey house located near a carpenter shop owned by Bill Little, the brother of George Little. This laundry shop was located in between Railroad Avenue and Grieg Street. He contracted washing linen for some of the hotels in town. Behind his laundry shop he had a vegetable garden in which he planted potatoes, carrots, onions and some Chinese vegetables such as bok choy (bai cai), and gai lan (jie lan). He used to sell his produce to Chinese cooks in the surrounding sawmills. He also sold fire-crackers to the kids at Halloween. Later, he left the laundry business and operated a café with his brother at the corner of Lakelse Avenue and Kalum Street. According to Bill McRae, Chinese old-timers used to visit the café and have a smoking session in the back room. Little Joe, however, would not sell cigarettes to young people. "When young people came to purchase cigarettes in the café," said McRae. "Joe would tell them, 'you go home, you too young, no smoke.' If someone came along who could not pay for his meal, Joe would feed him but say, 'You no pay, you pay next time.'" In the late 1930s, Joe left his business to his brother and no one knows where he went after that.

Wing Hing, also known as Long Tom, had his laundry in the same area as Joe's. The area where these two men operated their businesses was known as 'China Alley.' Hing was thin and tall but not as warm and friendly as Joe. When he wandered around town he always grasped his hands together and held them in his long sleeves across his abdomen. Because he was distant, children became curious about him and they often wanted to find out what he was doing in his shop. He used a hollow hot iron containing burning embers to iron clothing. This hot iron, with a lid latched on to prevent the embers from spilling, was attached on a spring suspended from a beam on the ceiling of his workroom. Before ironing, he sprinkled water on the clothing and then he pulled the hot iron down to smooth out the wrinkles. The spring prevented the hot iron from falling to the ground.

" I don't know what secrets these two Chinese laundry men had. Their wash always turned out sparkling white and fresh," commented Mamie Kerby. Apparently, all customers were happy with their work.

The two laundry men operated gambling dens in little rooms attached behind their buildings. Thus, they were not only competing for customers but also for gamblers. Men of different nationalities often sneaked into their dens to play solitaire, pokers, blackjack; they did not engage in fan-tan or other Chinese gambling games[1]. Some senior Canadians says that among Hing and Joe's frequent visitors was a police constable who loved to play a few hands of poker.

The Chinese farmers

Sah Hee and Jack Chow were two Chinese residents who made their living in vegetable marketing. Hee had his cultivated land in the Dutch Valley area in Terrace, whereas Jack Chow grew his vegetables and other produce on Braun's Island. Very few seniors can remember much about Sah Hee except that he had a green thumb and his garden was well planned and meticulous. Those who remember him admire his skills and success in gardening.

A good number of senior residents remember Jack Chow, who was a good neighbor to the Lambley family. When Geoff Lambley and his family moved to Terrace from Prince Rupert, they built a house on Haugland Avenue next to the Braun's Island Slough which adjoins Chow's farmland on Braun's Island. Chow built a small frame house on his 10 acres of cultivated land where he planted Chinese vegetables, potatoes, carrots, cabbages and onions.

He was a pleasant and friendly person who got along well with his neighbors. Don and Bob Cooper often used his house as lunchroom when they cut hay on their property. The Lambleys and Chows helped one another in their daily chores. When Geoff Lambley dug a cellar, Chow gave him a hand. Often the Lambley children helped Chow sort out potatoes. Whenever the Lambley children visited him, he cooked them Chinese meals, played Chinese records for them and taught them to count in Chinese. He was proud of his family back in China and often showed the Lambley children family photographs. When he visited the Lambleys, he gave them lichee nuts, candies and ginger from China. Once he brought Chinese dolls dressed in opera costumes to Freda Diesing and Bobby Perry, the Lambley girls. In summer when the Lambleys went swimming in the slough, Chow used to join them to have some fun, recalled Freda Diesing.

Everything went well until June 1936 when the Skeena River overflowed its banks causing a disastrous flood in the area. On June 6, 1936, the Province reported that "... the flood waters cut great gashes in the right-of-way between Terrace and Prince Rupert..." During the flood, Jack Chow and Geoff Lambley helped their neighbors move their chickens and cows and bring them from the Island to the Lambley's property. The flowing water was so vigorous that it ran into the Lambley cellar in no time. After the flood the water in the wells of Braun's Island became more alkaline which rendered the water less suitable for farming, so Chow sold his land to Sid Cooper and left for Prince Rupert.

Chow left Terrace because the flood affected him. Other Chinese left town because they wanted to find a better paying job elsewhere. Since their purpose of coming to the 'gold mountains' was to find their fortunes and to improve their lives as well as those of their loved ones at home, they naturally moved around the Skeena Valley to find better paying jobs. In reality, many had already left the area during the Great Depression and moved to Vancouver and Victoria where they could receive support from their countrymen. This occurrence created a void in the history of the Chinese immigrants in Terrace.

When Terrace was selected as an army base in World War II, the forest industries became active, especially in the harvesting of Sitka spruce for building airplanes. Roads were extended to all directions and bridges were built over rivers and creeks. Highway 16 was finally completed in 1944 connecting Terrace to Prince Rupert in the west and to Prince George in the southeast. It is unknown if all these activities had attracted Chinese immigrants to the area to look for work. After the war, army officers and soldiers departed turning Terrace back into a quiet town.

In 1946, the establishment of the Columbia Cellulose Company, a subsidiary of the Celanese Corporation of America, on Watson Island near Prince Rupert, motivated many people to migrate to Terrace. This pulp mill, now known as the Skeena Cellulose Corporation, required a large supply of wood chips for the manufacture of high alpha pulp. The need for forest products led to the establishment of more sawmills and other forestry companies, thus stimulating the development and growth of Terrace. Once again, sawmills and other forestry industries mushroomed in Terrace. All these activities attracted a large number of people to the area, including a number of Chinese families. Many Chinese Canadians went there to open restaurants, and they became the core members of the Chinese community in Terrace.

Sad Stories

In addition to these bits and pieces of Chinese immigrant history in Terrace, some sad stories have been discovered. According to Bill McRae, a knowledgeable senior, some labourers were killed during the construction of the GTP near Terrace. Their bodies were buried in a remote area near the railway track but their skeletons were exposed after a few years. That brought the RCMP and doctors to the scene to identify the remains. From the size and density of the bones, it was confirmed that some skeletons belonged to Russians while others were Chinese remains. The Russian community took care of the Russian remains, but no one could provide information about what happened to the Chinese skeletons.

Another incident took place in Lakelse Lake Resort where Mah Ling, an elderly Chinese cook, suddenly died of heart attack. In the summer of 1956, a group of businessmen spent their vacation at the resort. One evening, they went to the dining room for supper but the tables were not laid and no meal was in sight. So, one of them went to the kitchen to look for the cook and found him lying dead on the floor. The deceased Chinese cook was holding an unlit cigarette between his first and second fingers. One person in the group quickly went to Terrace and reported the case to the RCMP. While waiting, one of the other gentleman became agitated and paced up and down the dining room floor.

"I wish I had a cigarette," said the nervous man.

"Well, the dead man is holding one unlit in his hand," responded one of his friends. "If you are desperate you can take it from him."

"That remark made the nervous person even more fidgety," said Bill McRae.

Lastly is an open secret in Terrace regarding the killing of a Chinese man. Many long-time residents are aware of this incident but few want to talk about the assault of a Chinese man near the Silver Tips Chinese Restaurant at Lazelle Street in the early 1960s. The Chinese man was beaten to death while people watched.

"This incident took place before we came to Terrace," said Glenn Wong. "The victim happened to be in the wrong place at the wrong time. Apparently, the guy was drunk when he assaulted the Chinese man. It is a 'black spot' in the history of Terrace, At a time when the residents were making an effort not to discriminate against citizens of other national origins, that incident took place." Unfortunately no record of the case has been found.

However, a number of Chinese men bearing the surnames Wong and Lim had died in Terrace and were buried in the Kalum Cemetery between 1958 and 1970. According to the Vital Statistics Department, many of them died of old age or natural causes, but some were killed in accidents.[2]

The Wong Family

The Gim Restaurant on Park Avenue is one of the oldest and best-known Chinese restaurants in Terrace. Its owner, Gim Wong, came from the southern part of Guangdong in 1951. His father, who had left two wives in China and lived with one in Vancouver, sponsored him to immigrate to Canada. Once again, politics in China determined overseas family decisions. In 1950 when Mao Zedong initiated the Land Reform campaign, many Chinese people, including landlords and common folk who received remittances from relatives overseas, were branded as capitalists and were tortured and humiliated by the Chinese Government[3]. Under such circumstances Wong's father felt that it was safer for his son Gim to come to Canada. By that time, his two wives in China had died and no other family member remained in the village to look after Gim.

After Gim Wong arrived in British Columbia, he did not stay long with his father and the third wife in Vancouver. His father sent him to Endako to live with a friend and attend school there. There he stayed in a Chinese owned dormitory. One year later, he went to Prince George and attended Prince George Secondary School (PGSS).

In PGSS he was an active student. After school he devoted his time and energy to the production of the school year book, the *Northern Light*, for two years. He was an artist and produced a drawing of the former secondary school, the Byron Bing Secondary School, for the inner cover of the 1956 year book. In 1956-57 he was elected as treasurer of the Student Council. He was the artist again for the *Northern Light* that year. In June 1957 he graduated from the high school.

After graduation he went into partnership with Charlie Chow and operated the Sunrise Café in Hazelton. The partnership worked well and they did a thriving business. In 1958 he married Lena Chow, from Hong Kong, in Vancouver. Both the bride and the groom met for the first time on the day of their wedding, as it was an arranged marriage. After the wedding, Wong took his wife back to Hazelton and continued in the restaurant business. A couple of years later his partnership with Chow went sour.

"Charlie [Chow] was good man but his wife was rather disappointing," commented Glenn, the second son of Gim Wong. "Charlie's wife manipulated the situation in such a way that my father had to sell his share to her husband in 1963."

In the same year, Wong and his family left Hazelton and opened the Gim's Restaurant on Park Avenue in Terrace. The space for Gim's Restaurant was rented from Mr. Onstein. By that time, the Wongs had two boys, Albert and Glenn, in the family.

One day, as Albert was playing with a ball in the yard in front of their house, the young toddler ran after the ball as it rolled out to street without realizing that a truck was coming. It ran over him and killed him instantly. It was a devastating and painful experience for the Wongs.

Over the next few years the Wong couple added two more boys and a girl to their family. The Wong children went through the school system in Terrace from elementary to high school. While the children were in elementary school they had difficulty in learning and speaking English. The Wongs, especially Lena, spoke Cantonese to their children. They did not realize that using Chinese at home would affect the progress of their children in school. The elementary school, however, appointed a special instructor to teach them English. Everyday they spent half a day with the teacher in order to learn English.

"To get us exposed to the English language, the teacher allowed us to watch as many English films, and later, as many video tapes as we wanted to. We were allowed to read as many comic books as we liked in that class," said Glenn Wong.

The Gim's Restaurant - opened in Terrace in 1963.

Photo courtesy Anthony Yao.

To ensure that the Wong children would learn and speak English, the social services intervened and instructed the parents not to speak Chinese to their school aged children at home. It was pretty tough for the whole family.

Some neighbors also reported to the school authorities that the Wong children were neglected. Their parents appeared to have little time to supervise them and allowed the children to run around in the neighborhood. This allegation was brought to the attention of Social Services, which threatened to take the children away.

"My dad was furious when Social Services intervened. And my mother almost went into a seizure when she learned that her children would be taken away from her," said Glenn Wong.

Lena Wong simply could not understand why Social Services had issued such a warning. To her, both husband and wife had done their best in raising their children. They had provided the children with food, clothing and shelter. They always took the children with them to the restaurant whenever they went to work as was expected of a Chinese family.

"True, we spent lots of time in the restaurant, which we treated as home. Our house was just a place we slept at night. Every morning when we woke up we went to the restaurant to eat and play," remarked Glenn Wong.

These occurrences reveal the life of Chinese restaurant people in the past, and the traditional way of child raising in many Chinese homes. When the economy of British Columbia is strong, a good restaurant is busy from the hour it opens to the time it closes. The Gim Restaurant was the busiest café in town, and they usually worked more than twelve hours a day. The Wongs truly had no time to look after their children according to Canadian standards. However, they felt that their children were taken care of since they were not left alone at home. Further, it was a common practice in China, Hong Kong and Southeast Asia for parents to take their children with them to their shops. These children were not expected to stay in the shops all the time. They were allowed to wander around, go window-shopping and/or visit with their peers in the neighborhood. There was an inherent trust between parents and children.

The Wongs were no exception. They trusted that their children would behave themselves in the neighborhood when they went out of the restaurant. The children, too, understood the expectations of their parents and conducted themselves accordingly. So the children were allowed to leave the restaurant whenever they liked. Even Glenn Wong did not feel that he and his siblings were being mistreated or neglected. It was just the way of life in the Wong family, and in other Chinese business families as well.

"With that kind of freedom and trust, we had the opportunity to learn to be independent," said Glenn Wong. "If we did not like the restaurant food we had to cook our own meals either at home or in the restaurant. We did our own laundry and homework without any help or supervision from our parents. It really helped us to grow up."

However, Gim Wong realized that they were living in a western society and their children had to acquire English. Ultimately, he came to terms with the school and Social Services and spoke mainly English with his children at home. This also gave Lena a chance to practise English. Meanwhile, he employed more people to help in the kitchen and in the dining room, so that he could spend more time with his children. Whenever he could, he went shopping with his children, attended their sport tournaments and other school functions, as well as met with their teachers during parent-teacher nights in school. Later, he volunteered his time in the community by sponsoring a local children's hockey team and a junior soccer team. In 1971, he joined the Rotary Club and served with perfect attendance for twenty-four years. In 1985, he was presented with the Paul Harris Fellow Award for his continuous services and dedication. He was described as "dependable, conscientious and reliable, a man who never refused a task that was requested of him...[he was] the man behind the scenes...and never drew attention to himself."[4]

Throughout his life, Gim Wong had many triumphant moments. In 1978, he successfully built the new Gim's Restaurant on 4643 Park Avenue. It was an important occasion in his life. Despite the strike at the Natural Gas Company, the building was completed on time for the grand opening, which was attended by all the local dignitaries and his friends in Terrace. Another significant moment in his life was the day when he paid off the mortgages on the restaurant and the house.

"My dad celebrated the occasion with a drink even though he had a weak heart," said Glenn Wong.

As time went by the condition of Gim's heart deteriorated. In 1984, he went to Vancouver hospital for a bypass surgery. He recovered but twelve years later his heart failed. On July 19, 1996, he died, survived by his wife and four children. It was his wish to be buried with Albert, his first child. So, arrangements were made to exhume the bones of Albert from the Terrace cemetery to be reburied with Gim in Vancouver.

After Gim Wong passed away, Lena took over the business and has operated the restaurant since then. Even when her husband was alive, she devoted a great deal of her time and energy to the business. She preferred to look after the business because she felt that her English was not good enough to get involved with the activities of her children in school and in their social activities. She gave her husband the opportunity to be with the children at school functions and to get involved in the community. She also felt that she had to look after the restaurant when her husband went out.

"My mom never went with us to any of our school functions," said Glenn Wong. "She did not even attend our valedictory ceremonies when we graduated from high school. Only if she knew how much we wanted her to be with us at these important occasions."

All the Wong children went on to get a post-secondary education and turned out to be good and successful citizens. Their daughter Diane is a teacher at the Terrace campus of the Northwest Community College. She is married and occasionally goes back to help her mother in the restaurant. Glenn, who went to the Cariboo College in Kamloops and then transferred to the British Columbia Institute of Technology (BCIT), obtained a diploma in chemical science. After graduation, he worked as a gold assayer (a chemical engineer who determines the amount of gold in a sample of raw dirt) with the Mosquito Quartz Mine in Wells. He volunteered his services to the Barkerville Historical Park while in Wells. He went through all the back issues of the *Cariboo Sentinel*, cataloguing and indexing articles relating to the early Chinese. He also gave his time as a tourist guide in the Chinatown of Barkerville. Presently, he is the manager of the Pacific Environmental Consulting and Occupational Hygiene Services Ltd. in Prince George, a company which performs environmental audits.

Although he is a first generation of Chinese Canadians, he knows many Chinese customs and traditions.

"In our home my mum and grandparents have insisted that we observe and maintain Chinese customs," stated Glenn Wong. "We practise the tea serving ceremony in a wedding and keep the custom of wearing red on happy occasions such as a wedding, Full Moon of a new born child, and other occasions. We also give red packets to children on Chinese New Year and on their birthdays. We wear jute, black or white for a funeral. We are taught and constantly reminded to show respect and care for the senior folks."

'Full Moon' refers to the first month after a child is born. It is an important event in a Chinese family, who usually celebrate the occasion by providing a big feast as well as distributing red eggs and pickled ginger to relatives and friends.

Although the Wongs practice no religion, Lena is a staunch worshipper of Guan Yin, the Goddess of Mercy. She burns incense to this deity everyday. The Wongs also observe Qing Ming every year. During Qing Ming they go to the graveyard, clean the tombs, place flowers on the Chinese graves and burn incense. They usually bring along fruits and food, and at times, a whole roast pig for the ritual. After they finish the ritual at the cemetery, they repeat the same procedure at the family altar. Then they distribute the roast pork to Chinese families in town and have a big feast at home.

Gim Wong and his family have certainly made their marks in the history of Terrace, as good citizens well-integrated into Canadian society. Now the Wong children are truly Chinese Canadians in that they have inherited the positive aspects of Chinese cultures but live their lives like other Canadians.

Other Chinese families

The Locke family has been in Terrace for more than 30 years. Sam Locke, the owner of the Chop Suey Garden, came from the Xin An Village in Taishan County. In 1952, Sam arrived in British Columbia and he went to Prince George to work in the Majestic Café. In Prince George, he met Gim Wong and their friendship grew. In 1963, he went to Hong Kong and married Susie, who received her early education at the Nan Yang Village, and later attended high school in Guangzhou. After her graduation from high school, she went to Hong Kong where she lived for eleven years.

Shortly after the birth of their first daughter, Sam returned to Terrace and worked in Gim's restaurant. In 1967, he opened the Chop Suey Garden on 4430 Greig Avenue, and sent for his family to join him. When Susie arrived with her daughter, she did not go out to the restaurant to help her husband. Instead she spent 10 years as a housewife and a mother. Over the years the Lockes added three more girls and one boy to the family. When the children were young, Susie taught them Chinese heritage and language at home.

"When I first came to Terrace, I found the town too quiet for my liking," said Susie. "I was used to living in big cities like Guangzhou and Hong Kong where life is colorful and exciting. I felt rather lonesome and lost in this town at the beginning. Luckily my children kept me busy."

As time went by, she became adjusted to the new environment and found friends in Terrace. Her children went through the school system in Terrace. Their eldest daughter is a teacher in Terrace and the third daughter works as a secretary at the Terrace Town Hall. Two other daughters are working in the Lower mainland while her youngest son is helping his father in the restaurant business.

Other Chinese families include the Yees of the Polly Café, the Lees of the Shan Yan Restaurant and the Yips of the Yip Chi Café. These Chinese families, as well as the Wongs and Lockes, form the core of the Chinese Canadian community. Over the years, numerous Chinese cooks have come to Terrace to work in these Chinese restaurants. Roy Wong, a schoolteacher, taught in Terrace for some time. Later, he and his wife, Elaine, moved to Coquitlam. Another Charlie Chow, a logger in Terrace, married a white woman, but they left for Port Coquitlam after a few years.

Festivals

Since the Chinese community of Terrace consists of people from villages in the southern part of Guangdong and Hong Kong, one would expect them to put great emphasis on the celebration of Chinese New Year, the most important Chinese festival. Surprisingly, none of the families has celebrated the occasion on a grand scale or collectively put on a showcase for the community. In their private homes they burn incense and offer flowers to their ancestors to mark the day.

"We restaurant people have only two days off in a year, Christmas and Boxing Day," said Sam Locke. "During Chinese New Year the Chinese restaurants remain open. We just do not have time to get together for the occasion."

"The first ten years or so after we settled here, we did not even know Chinese New Year had arrived," added Susie Locke. "We did not have a Chinese calendar to remind us of the occasion. It has been only in the last two decades that we have been able to get a Chinese calendar."

However, 15 years ago the Chinese community raised some money and invited the Lion Dance Troupe from Prince Rupert to perform in all the Chinese restaurants. That was the only time they have held a traditional celebration as a Chinese community. The Lion Dance attracted many people in Terrace, who came out to watch the colourful performance.

Like other Canadians, they celebrate Christmas with zeal. They decorate their homes and shops with Christmas trees and ornaments, as well as send greeting cards to friends and relatives. During Christmas season the restaurant owners often give presents to their employees as a token of appreciation, and invite them to a Christmas party. On Christmas Day morning, each family opens their presents. Then they have breakfast together. By noon they usually gather together in one of the restaurants and visit with each other. The men play mahjong, with a break at dinnertime, until the next morning when their wives, who left after the banquet, phone and remind them to come home.

In the restaurant, the women catch up on the latest news in each family, and to compare the achievements of their children in school and other endeavors. Some women help the cooks in the kitchen to prepare the big banquet for the evening. In the banquet they have not only turkey with delicious stuffing but also a 10-course Chinese meal. It is a day to get drunk and be merry. The Chinese children also have a once-in-a-year opportunity to meet and play with one another as a group of Chinese Canadians.

On Boxing Day, everyone sleeps in until noon. In the late afternoon, the restaurant workers go to their employers' homes. There they watch television, catch up with the latest news about their friends and relatives in other cities or in China, and exchange gossip about Chinese movie stars. These are the two days that restaurant people are able to relax and unwind.

So far, this sketch constitutes the history of Chinese settlement in Terrace. No records remain of any associations or of communal celebrations. Many seniors in the community have noted that most of the Chinese single men were fond of children, thus illustrating the loneliness and the longing for family life of the early Chinese immigrants.

Chapter Seven

SMITHERS

Little Switzerland

Smithers, a beautiful and peaceful town, is located at the foot of the Hudson Bay Mountain in the Bulkley Valley. It is 334 kilometres east of Prince Rupert and 356 kilometres northwest of Prince George. The mountain slopes are a skiing haven in winter and the trails at its foot offer excellent hiking in summer. The streams and lakes nearby are ideal places for fishing and picnicking. The mountainous region with its waterfalls creates an alpine atmosphere similar to that of a European country, hence the name, "Little Switzerland."

The surrounding mountains, including the Babine Mountain to the east, contain invaluable timbers that provide raw materials for forest industries such as logging, sawmills and railroad tie making. The Bulkley Valley is endowed with fertile soil for agriculture. During the era of constructing an overland telegraph line connecting North America to Europe, Thomas Elwyn, a magistrate of the Telegraph Company, reached the Bulkley Valley around 1866. He commented that "the land between McClure Lake and Morricetown could support all the crops in north England.[1]"

The nearby grasslands support beef cattle and dairy herds. Both kinds of cattle roam the pastures in summer and are fed hay during winter months but supplemental wheat and oats are added to the diet for the dairy herds. Numerous milk-processing plants operated in Smithers in the early days, but were relocated to Prince George about twenty-five years ago. Today, one milk-processing plant is still operating in Telkwa, a town about twelve kilometres south of Smithers.

Large deposits of coal, silver, gold, copper, molybdenum and other minerals can be found in the area surrounding Smithers. The Cronin Mine, east of Smithers, began mining for silver, copper, lead and zinc in the 1900s. The

Bulkley Colliers excavated coal at Telkwa from 1918 to 1982. There were several mining companies such as the Dome Mining Company, the Golden Bear Company and others, many of which employed Chinese workers[2]. In short, Smithers possesses not only great charms but also enormous natural resources.

This town is named after Sir Alfred Waldron Smithers, the chairman of the Grand Trunk Railway Board. By 1913 the construction of the Grand Trunk Pacific Railway had reached Hazelton, and a site was needed to erect a divisional station to connect Prince Rupert to Prince George. At first, Hubert, a town located about fourteen kilometres east of Telkwa, was selected for the divisional station. It was an ideal place because the land is flat but not swampy. However, the GTP Company could not secure lands around Hubert, as many speculators had already bought up the land and demanded high prices for their properties.

Telkwa was considered as the next possible site, but the provincial Government disapproved of the selection because that route would follow the bank of the Telkwa River and then proceed along on the bank of the Copper River to reach Prince Rupert. Following that direction would interfere with the development of most agricultural and mining lands in the Bulkley Valley[3].

Finally, Smithers became the choice for the divisional station. It was not a very good option as the area then was a swamp. Water had to be drained and the ground had to be filled with boulders and rocks before laying any railway tracks. Poles had to be driven into muddy ground to give support and reinforcement to the buildings in the area between Railroad Avenue and Broadway South.

"Although I came to Smithers in 1965, the roads and streets were still soft and wobbly in spring," remarked Jim Woo, former owner of the Northern Star Cafe.

Finally, Smithers was incorporated as a village in 1921 and as a town in 1967. Since then the town has been greatly improved with paved roads and a well-planned town-site.

The Early Chinese immigrants

As difficult as it may be to believe, not many Chinese labourers were employed in the construction of the GTP. At that time, the British Columbia Government, the labour unions, and all the anti-Chinese organizations were dead against the GTP Company employing any Chinese labourers. Even on

Kaien Island near Prince Rupert, where the GTP began its construction in 1906, the number of Chinese people employed in the company was about forty-two between 1906 and 1909. A GTP agent explained that "the Asians had simply 'drifted in' and were doing only menial work... round the table and cleaning dishes"[4]. At that time, only Chinese cooks were working in the railway camps at Smithers, but some of them joined railroad gangs as the construction proceeded.

Between 1920 and 1923, some Chinese names appeared in the Smithers County Court records dealing with small debt claims. They were Woo Lee, Wong Chong, Jim Sing Set, and Chow Kwong who claimed that the Cronin Mine and the Dome Mountain Gold Mining Company, for which they worked, owned them wages. This evidences indicates that some Chinese immigrants were in the vicinity. Senior citizens in Smithers remember meeting some Chinese immigrants in the late 1920s.

"I started working in the post office in 1929. I noticed that many Chinese men came to the post office to send money home," said Ruby Hoskins. "When they came, we knew that it was the end of the month. They certainly loved and looked after their families in China because they often sent large sums of money home. They could not speak English but they sure could make us understand them."

According to the 1931 Canadian Census, the total population of Smithers consisted of 1000 people including 25 Asians of Japanese and Chinese descent. The Census did not specify ethnic origin, and there is speculation that more Chinese immigrants were living in Smithers but were not recorded.

"Being single men, the early Chinese immigrants were very mobile," commented Jim Woo. "We can assume that they were not at home when the census was taken. They often went to work in the nearby villages such as Aldermere or Telkwa." However, memories of the early Chinese settlers are clear, if not the actual number living here.

"Among the Chinese old-timers Mah Yoke Tong was the kindest person I have ever met," remarked Gordon Hetherington, a well-known veteran and hockey player in Smithers. "He did more good in Smithers than anyone I can think of in his time." Mah was indeed well known and respected in Smithers, according to many old-timers.

Mah Yoke Tong and His Extended Family

Mah Yoke Tong came from Bai Sha Tong village in Taishan county, Guangdong. No one knows the exact date he left China or what he did prior to settling in Smithers except that he had worked in Aldermere and Telkwa. He came to Smithers around 1915 and operated a bakery store, located at the corner of Main Street and First Avenue. Once Mah settled in Smithers he never left except to take trips to Telkwa occasionally. He owned and operated the bakery for more than 40 years.

Everyone remembers the good bread and delicious pastries Mah produced. Every Tuesday he produced a special rye bread that his customers loved. They would come to the bakery early and buy the hot, crisp bread to take home. The rye loaves were so good that they were sold out as soon as they were taken from the oven.

"He also made the best doughnuts," said Ruby Hoskin.

"I loved the cookies he made," commented Chuck Morris, a retired salesman who traveled extensively from Vanderhoof to Hazleton for more than twenty-five years. He knew many of the Chinese people in the area.

"His raisin cookies were very special. Each one was about six inches in diameter," added Pat McCammon, a daughter of Ernie Hann, a pioneer who has lived in Smithers since the incorporation of the village.

"He used to trim the edges of raisin cookies and put the trimmings in a tray on his counter. We kids could go in any time to help ourselves to the trimmings," said Wilfred Watson, a senior citizen, who has retired from his grocery business. "As kids, whenever we had a few cents, we often went to the bakery for a treat."

"We had a grocery store in the early days. We kids used to take the empty boxes to the baker. Every time we went there, we were given a choice either to take a quarter or to have a cream puff. We always chose the cream puff," stated Diantree Riffel, another senior citizen in Smithers.

"He was a smart and efficient businessman," said Gordon Hetherington. "He sold his white bread at a quarter for three loaves but at ten cents per loaf. He expected his customers to come and buy three loaves at a time because that was cheaper. Therefore, he always put three loaves of bread in a brown paper bag ready for his customers."

Mah loved his trade and devoted his time to baking. Everyday he prepared the ingredients and then kneaded the dough in the evening. Sometimes, while waiting for the dough to rise, he would go to Chinatown to play cards with his friends. At that time the so-called Chinatown was located in the area between Railroad and Broadway south where most of the Chinese people lived.

When he returned after his visit to Chinatown, he would sleep on a wooden bench near the heater and wake up in time to start the fire. He used wood, and later coal, as a source of heat for baking. In his time there were no thermostats to regulate the temperature needed for the various types of baking. As he had been in the trade for a long time, he had developed the skill of producing the right temperature by feeding exactly the right amount of wood to the stove and leaving an appropriate quantity of embers to produce the required heat.

Wilfred Watson and Cris Agnew had a contract with Mah to cut wood for the bakery. Mah purchased the wood from farmers who usually delivered them in sixteen feet lengths. These two young men cut the wood to about twenty inches length to fit his stove. They also split the wood into appropriate sizes and piled them.

"It was a steady job," said Wilfred Watson, " We went there to cut wood for him everyday after school until Bilf Teach set up a buzz-saw and put us out of business."

At Halloween, children would call at the bakery first because they were certain to get some goodies from the baker. He supported every town project and donated generously to any activities involving young people. Wherever there was a game or match between Smithers' schools and other districts, he would take time off to cheer and support his home team. At the end of the game or match, the home team members would burst through the door of the bakery to get their share of fresh doughnuts reserved for them. He would never turn away anyone who canvassed for charity.[5] During the Great Depression people were not turned away hungry when they called at the bakery store.

In the late 1940s, lumber was in big demand and about fifty sawmills were established in the surrounding villages such as Moricetown and Houston. During winter all these sawmills were shut down, leaving many lonely men without families. During Christmas day no restaurant was open and these workers had no place to eat unless they had stocked up a big supply of cheese, crackers and garlic sausages. One Christmas, Watson and his wife Stella, together with his aunt, Nellie Downey and other friends, decided to host a Christmas dinner in a large hotel for these poor men. In that event Mah was asked to roast turkeys for the dinner party. He also donated pastries and cookies to the party. After the Christmas dinner, he became a member of that charitable group for years.

Although no one had heard him talking about his family in China, he helped his nephew and grandsons to immigrate to Canada. In 1922, Mah sponsored his nephew Mah Wing Shek, known as Little Wing by many in town, to come over and help him in his bakery. While Little Wing was in Smithers he attended school with Jack Chapman and Wilfred Watson.

According to these two seniors, Little Wing was a talented artist.

"Little Wing liked to draw portraits of his classmates on the blackboard in the classroom," commented Watson, "He was a likeable person, always smiling and often laughing."

"I used to operate a restaurant in this town," said Vera Heggie. "When I went to the baker to buy bread I often gave them loose change. Instead of counting the coins, Little Wing weighed them on a scale. It always came out to be the right amount."

In Mah's ledger he recorded the different kinds of goodies he baked. His products included breads, rolled buns, doughnuts, rock or plain scones, fruit-cakes, fruit pies, cream puffs and cookies. He also entered the cost of the raw materials, the selling prices of all the items, the names of the customers to whom he had given credit and the amounts owing to him. These entries were written in Chinese characters until 1940 and then in English up to 1954. Perhaps his nephew, Little Wing, recorded the later entries in the ledger.

In the early fifties, Little Wing went home to get married and brought his wife back. She was the first Chinese woman to arrive in Smithers. Later, Mah also sponsored his two grandsons, Ken and Joe Mah to Canada and sent them to school in Smithers.

On February 11, 1955, Mah Yoke Tong passed away at the age of 84 and was buried in the Smithers Cemetery. Many people attended his funeral. At the gate of the cemetery all those who went to the funeral were given a small brown envelope containing a candy and a coin, a Chinese custom practised by many Chinese Canadians. It represents an acknowledgement from the family of the deceased and their good wishes to all those who attend the funeral.

From 1955 Little Wing operated the bakery with help from his two cousins until it was shut down in the 1960s. Then all of them moved to Burnaby. According to Ken Kwan the owner of the Twin Valley Motor Inn, Little Wing died in the late 1980s.

Some other Chinese Old-timers

Some senior citizens, especially the members of the Hann family, fondly remembered Joe Suey, an old Chinese man. Mrs. Addie Hann, a hundred-year-old senior citizen, often talks about Joe Suey with her daughter, Pat McCammon. During the 1930s, Joe lived in a tiny log cabin and had a vegetable garden near Railroad Avenue on the west side of town. He raised pigs near Chicken Creek, a place next to the Wildwood subdivision bordering the present golf course.

He fed the pigs with slops collected from private homes and restaurants. Mrs. Hann kept all her peelings and other food remains in pails and gave them to Joe when he came around every two days. On such a day the Hann children would yell, "Here comes Joe, Mother!" when they spotted him at a distance. At times, one of the children would take the pails to him when he arrived at the door. He always remarked that Mrs. Hann had so many good children as they handed him the pails.

Old Joe had a cart made of two bicycle wheels with a platform in between on which he kept his tins and barrels for collecting slops The platform was extended with two poles on one end to form the handles of a wheelbarrow. Everyday he would push this homemade wheelbarrow around town to collect slops. In addition, he fed his pigs with barley, oats and wheat so that the animals would produce firm meat. All together, he had about twenty-five to thirty pigs, but he kept them separated. The mature pigs would be kept in one pen while the young were all kept in another big pen. The mature pigs were taken to the local butcher for slaughtering, and the Watson Grocery store retailed the pork. In summer Old Joe would sell the produce from his vegetable garden door to door.

"He was a very a generous man who often gave his customers more than their money's worth when they bought produce from him," remarked Pat McCammon. This practice is still very common among hawkers and peddlers in China, Taiwan and Southeast Asia. Most Chinese hawkers usually give their customers a stalk of green onion or a piece of small ginger as a token of appreciation. They believe that a little gift goes a long way because the customers remember them and deal with them when they come around the next time.

Old Joe used to give the Hanns lily bulbs just before Christmas and told them to grow these bulbs in bowls of pebbles filled with water. In January the lilies would bloom. He did not stay in Smithers for long though. Before World War II he sold his property and moved to Toronto.

Chung Kee, the owner of a laundry shop, is also fondly remembered in Smithers. His business was located on Broadway South next to the Smithers Hotel. He was a good laundry man and his customers were happy with his service. He also roasted and sold the most delicious peanuts in town.

"When I was young I used to collect and sell beer bottles. As soon as I made a quarter I would go to Chung Kee to buy his tasty peanuts," said Gordon Hetherington. "He was generous, too, for he usually gave me more peanuts than my money's worth."

Many Chinese grandparents in traditional homes still make these "roasted"

Irish's cabin along the Finlay River.
Photo courtesy Bill & Helene MacRae

peanuts. In truth, they do not roast the peanuts in an oven but fry them in a wok using low heat. First, they remove the shells from the nuts. Then they put the nuts with skins attached into a wok and stir them constantly. When the skins crack open to expose the light brown nuts, they add a little oil and sprinkle some salt on the nuts. They stir the mixture thoroughly for five to ten minutes at low heat so that the nuts absorb the salty flavour. Then the nuts can be spooned out to serve, but they taste best when they are cool.

In 1936, a huge fire burnt down the Smithers Hotel and its neighbourhood. That fire must have affected the Chung Kee Laundry because no one saw him after. Perhaps he left town and went somewhere else to look for work.

Bang King or "Irish" was a cook in one of the GTP camps at Smithers. After the completion of the GTP line, Irish went to Manson Creek to pan for gold. Many in old Hazelton and Smithers became acquainted with him. He was a tall man with a commanding personality and often brushed aside minor incidents with laughter. Wherever he went, he took his dog Tippy with him.

In Smithers he owned the OK Café that was located at Broadway off Main Street, and operated the restaurant himself during winter. In the summer he left his business to his employees and walked to Manson Creek to placer mine. He was known as the "god father" of the Chinese people in Bulkley

The Bulkley Valley Hotel staff and its most famous cook, Moon (extreme right), 1939.
Photo courtesy Maude Pederson

Valley because he had helped many Chinese immigrants to find work. He also loaned money to his countrymen in China to pay the head tax in order to come to Canada. In 1945 his café was burned down together with the eight other buildings in the block. It was one of the biggest fires in the history of Smithers with losses estimated at about $150,000.00. After the fire no one saw "Irish" in Smithers again.

Another Chinese man fondly remembered is Moon, who came to Smithers from Terrace in the 1930s. He was a well-regarded cook in the Bulkley Hotel then owned by Geo Orchard. The Bulkley Hotel was located on the Main Street directly facing the Alfred Horn, the symbol of Smithers. Moon was famous for his fast cooking. He had a large stove with two big ovens in his kitchen. He could cook about 75 to 100 T-bones steaks in the ovens at one time and whip up a banquet for 100 people within a couple of hours. His name, Moon, means "full" in Cantonese, which is a symbol of prosperity and contentment.

"Nowadays, no one can cook as fast as Moon did," said Maude Pederson, who was a waitress in the restaurant then.

Like most restaurants in the area at the time, Moon's used wood as fuel. Business was so brisk that Moon contracted young Gordon Williams, now a well-known resident in Smithers, to supply wood for cooking. Moon left Smithers for a short period and returned to work for the Heggies in the Northern Star Café. A few years later he died of cancer and was buried in Smithers.

Ah Fong or "Papa Fong" was another familiar Chinese man who operated a café on Main Street. He escaped the big fire in 1945 because he sold the restaurant shortly before the fire. Then he moved to a small cabin behind Wing's Café, a restaurant owned and operated by Kwan Wing who was commonly known as "Big Wing." In the cabin Fong lived with Mickey Delare, an old Irishman, for many years. Both Fong and Delare bootlegged and seemed to make a fair living.

"After hockey practices some of us would go Papa Fong's cabin for a few hot rums," said Wilfred Watson. "He always supported our hockey team. I remember him, wearing a Mackinaw coat pulled tight around his body, watching our games from a snow bank. He was friendly and gave each member of the team a nickname."

During hunting season Papa Fong went grouse shooting. When he caught a few birds, he brought them to the baker Mah to make a big pot of grouse soup with winter melon to treat their friends, including Caucasians. In his spare time Fong loved to smoke tobacco leaves in his homemade bamboo pipe. Obsolete now, the pipe was made up of a bamboo stem about three-feet long with the partitions inside the stem removed except for one near the end.

A Chinese man smoking a Chinese water pipe.

Photo courtesy Harry Low.

A hole was drilled on the side of the bamboo stem near the middle. A shorter and thinner piece of hollow bamboo was sealed tightly in the hole. Water was added to the large bamboo pipe until it reached just above the smaller pipe. When a person wanted to smoke, he put shredded tobacco leaves in the open end of the small pipe, lit them up and inhaled from the top of the large pipe. The water filtered and removed the tar. At the end of smoking, the brownish water containing tobacco tar was drained away. Fresh water was added to the pipe whenever the person wanted to smoke again.

Although some people liked Fong, many avoided his company. One Canadian senior said that Fong often brought prostitutes from other towns into the community. Many senior citizens prefer not to mention his involvment in prostitution. As his enterprises triggered more than a little resentment among the residents of Smithers, no one remembers when he left town.

The Chinese Canadians

In 1956, Kwan Wing, the owner of the Wing's Café, sponsored his grandson, Ken Kwan to immigrate to Canada. When Kwan junior arrived he was only 15 years old. Ken attended school in Smithers for two years and then went to Vancouver, Calgary and finally the United States. In 1962, he went to Hong Kong to get married and returned with his wife to Smithers. Over the years they have raised five sons and one daughter.

Shortly after Ken and his wife returned to Smithers Big Wing died, leaving the restaurant to the grandson. Later, Ken sold the property and started his own business, the Carousel Drive-in at the present location near Highway 16. He worked hard and gradually expanded his business to include a cold beer and wine store as well as hotel facilities. His business is now known as the Twin Valley Motor Inn. His wife, his eldest son and his daughter are helping him in his business. The other sons are in the Lower mainland except one, who is attending university in Alberta. Though he has been away from China for many years, he still retains his sentiment for his homeland.

"I always remind my children of their roots," said Ken Kwan. "A few years ago I took them back to China and gave them a chance to see how the Chinese people lived there. When they were young they did not have the opportunity to go to Chinese school to learn about the Chinese language and culture. The Chinese population in this town has always been small. We simply do not have the resources and time to establish a Chinese school in this community. When my children were young they were busy, too. They had many extracurricular activities in school and had to help out in the restaurant on weekends. However, we tried our best to observe some of the Chinese festivals at home. During the festive seasons we often celebrated the occasions together with other Chinese families in town and from both New and Old Hazleton. This was the way we introduced the Chinese culture to our children."

Jim Woo, another well-known Chinese resident in Smithers, agrees with Kwan. A small Chinese community is limited in finding resources to preserve the Chinese heritage and language, or to take part in Chinese rituals with other Chinese. Woo came to Canada in 1951 for a family reunion, but had another reason for emigrating from China.

"In 1950 the Korean War was on," said Woo. "I was attending school in Kaiping at the time. We students received a lot of propaganda from the Chinese authorities saying that the United States was using North Korea as a stepping stone. Once North Korea was conquered the next target would be China. The authorities then urged the young people to enlist in the armed force. It was scary for us to think that another world war would begin.

"After receiving that message, many students in my school voluntarily enlisted in the armed force. In our school we had about 1700 students. All of sudden half of them were gone! My parents, of course, were worried. My father who was in Canada sent for me immediately after learning about the situation from my mother. As a filial son, I had to obey my parents and fulfil their wishes. My mother and sister remained in China when I left home. They came to Canada a couple of years later," Woo continued.

In 1951 he landed in Saskatoon where his father had a restaurant. After he arrived he went to school in Saskatoon and helped his father to operate the restaurant until 1962. Two years later, Woo went to Hong Kong to get married and returned to Canada soon after. He went to Prince George to work while making arrangements for his wife to join him. In 1965 they came to Smithers and bought the Northern Star Restaurant from the Heggies. Both husband and wife operated the restaurant until 1995.

"Having been in the restaurant business for about 40 years–30 years here and 10 years in Saskatchewan–I really feel tired," commented Woo. "Restaurant business is time consuming and energy draining. It is not that we do not want to make money but that kind of money is too hard earned."

After a short pause he continued, with humor and self-satisfaction, saying, "Come to think of it, I have been a millionaire! I have raised four children and sent them to college and university for education. Roughly speaking I have invested about a quarter of a million dollars in each of them. I do not regret it because I know I have made good investments. That kind of investments will never make me lose anything, but will gain me love and understanding from my children."

"We have two grandchildren now, too, " adds Mrs. Woo happily

The Way It Is

Finally, the story of Chinese settlement in Smithers is recorded from the memories of senior citizens. They are not tales of adventures involving the migration of large groups of people but rather stories of individuals gradually trickling into town and leaving their marks there. These stories revealed the different background and the way of life of the Chinese, both Canadian and immigrant.

They were humble, simple and hard working folk who just wanted to get on with their lives. If in the early 1900s anti-Chinese sentiment had not existed in BC and the Chinese immigrants had been allowed to take on any employment, many Chinese immigrants would have settled in Smithers and in other smaller towns in the Bulkley Valley. The enforcement of the Chinese Exclusion Act kept the Chinese away from communities where white people predominated. Consequently, the Chinese immigrants moved around the Bulkley Valley instead of settling down in one place. If early journalists had taken more interest in recording Chinese activities and settlement, our history would be more comprehensive.

Luckily, those Chinese Canadians who settled in Smithers and the surrounding communities found life agreeable. They attempted to integrate into western society, and gained respect and appreciation among those who associated with them.

"All the Chinese people I met in the Bulkley Valley are honest and friendly people. They are a group of honorable citizens," commented Chuck Morris.

By the same token the Chinese Canadians who live in Smithers have also expressed their comfort in and appreciation of the community.

"We are happy living in Smithers," said Jim Woo. "The people here are friendly and understanding. We have no problem communicating with them. We also love the environment here. It is so peaceful living in the area where the mountains form the backdrop and the parks and lakes nearby allow people to appreciate the beauty of nature."

Over the years the Chinese residents in Smithers have contributed to the whole community. Mah Yoke Tong was noted for his support of many town projects and his nephew, Mah Wing Shek, as well as Jim Woo attempted to integrate into Canadian society. Although the actions of these Chinese may appear insignificant, they left lasting impressions on those who benefited from their kindness and generosity. It is encouraging to find that Canadians with different backgrounds can live in harmony and accept one another regardless of their color, racial origin or creed. Perhaps the only regret is that the Chinese Canadians in Smithers are unable to share their culture with others due to the small population and lack of resources.

Chapter Eight

KITIMAT

An Industrial District

The town of Kitimat lies on an alluvial plain at the end of the Kitimat Arm of the Douglas Channel. It is about 70 kilometres south of Terrace, and can be reached by road, air or sea. It has a deep-sea harbour and several private docks for ships to embark from and to unload their cargoes. The Kitimaat River, discharging its water in the Arm, is a migratory route for the various species of Pacific salmon returning to their spawning grounds.

White adventurers, missionaries and settlers reached the area as early as the 1790s. In 1833, the Hudson's Bay Company established its trading post at Fort McLoughlin, a place about 250 kilometers south of the native village of Kitimaat. The Tsimpshians and the Kwakiutl natives came to the area about 3000 years ago when they were searching for hunting and fishing grounds.[1] Eventually they formed a well-organized and independent community rich in art and music. In 1907, the Grand Trunk Pacific Railway (GTP) was supposed to connect Hazelton to Kitimaat Village, so that supplies for railway construction could be delivered from Kitamaat to the GTP main line on the north bank of the Skeena River. In 1923, the British Columbia Legislature passed a special act to incorporate the whole area as a district.[2]

Essentially this is a district of industries. A steel plant, a newsprint mill, a chemical factory and an oxygen producing plant were already in the district before the establishment of the three main companies, Alcan Smelters, Eurocan Paper and Pulp and Methanex/Pacific Ammonia. In 1951, McNeely Dubose, the vice-president of the Aluminium Company of Canada Ltd., Montreal, came to British Columbia to find a possible site for an aluminum smelter.[3] Dubose selected Kitimat as the site because cargo ships could enter into its deep sea harbour. The dock facilities would enable raw materials such as bauxite, pitch and coke from foreign countries to be delivered to the smelter for the extraction of aluminum. The first batch of aluminum ingots was produced in 1954. The establishment of the Alcan Smelters and Chemical Ltd. offered jobs to many people, including a good number of Chinese Canadians. Currently, the Chinese population is estimated as slightly more than 150 people, but two-thirds of the men are employees of Alcan. Some Chinese engineers and tradesmen are also working in the Eurocan and Methanex plants. Other Chinese Canadians include professionals and merchants in town.

Chinese Businesses

David Chow was the first Chinese Canadian to settle in Kitimat. Prior to arriving in Kitimat, Chow came alone from Guangzhou in 1910 and went to Trail to operate the Blue Bird Café. He then moved to Prince Rupert where he opened the Commodore Café. In 1953, the Alcan management, the Sheardown Brothers of Prince Rupert and Chow teamed up to establish the Helen Café at the Anderson Creek Camp, where the original construction camp was. The Alcan Company erected the building for the café next to the recreation hall. The Sheardown Brothers installed the equipment, and Chow operated the restaurant. Business in the café was brisk and thriving. The *Kitimat Ingot*, an Alcan newspaper, reported that "in the summer of 1955 an average of 3000 customers patronized the Helen Café daily". The *Ingot* also stated that most evenings people had to line up for a table when they went there for dinner. In 1956 the Helen Café catered its first banquet for the Kitimat Ladies' Social Club, attended by more than 70 women.

During the Alcan Smelters construction period, many trailers were set up at the campsite to accommodate company officers, construction workers and their families. Many of these families had children who had been deprived of ice cream, candy bars, chocolates and sweets for months since they moved into Kitimat. The opening of Helen Café was a joy to these kids for they could, once again, buy chocolates and candies to satisfy their cravings. During weekends, large crowds of youngsters would line up at the Helen Café to buy their favourite snacks.

In 1957, Chow moved the Helen Café to the centre of the Kitimat townsite. The new building and modern facilities cost him about $100,000. When the new Helen Café launched its grand opening, it was a triumphant moment for Chow. Many dignitaries and local people attended the event, and they were invited to a banquet. One of the main attractions of the new restaurant was a large mural in the dinning room showing the various stages of aluminum production in the smelter and the Kemano power generation plant which supplied the smelter with electricity. The mural was removed after Chow retired in 1971. Today, it can be found in the CAW Union Hall at 234 Enterprise Avenue. The restaurant was sold to a new owner who changed its name to Caruso Restaurant. Since Chow was the first Chinese resident in Kitimat, almost every Alcan employee knew him and he was nicknamed "the Kitimat Kid." One of his hobbies was to collect exotic coins. At the end of the day when he closed his till, he would look at all the coins and keep the unusual ones. In the community, he was an active member of the Kitimat Chamber of Commerce. On July 1, 1971, a banquet was held in his honor recognizing him as one of the six founding members of the organization.

"Kitimat has been a wonderful community in which to work and live...the people have been very kind and thoughtful," said Chow during an interview by the Kitimat newspaper the *Northern Sentinel* in 1971. Soon afterward he left town. Some of his friends said that he went back to China.

Another long-time Chinese resident of Kitimat is Bill Mah Hua Xin who came from Taishan county in Guangdong. In 1953, Mah's father sponsored him to Canada. He spent a year in Vancouver before he came up to Kitimat to work for David Chow at the Helen Café. He worked there for 32 months, and then went to Hong Kong to get married. In 1958, he came back with his wife and worked in another restaurant owned by a white Canadian. Their first child Peter was born in Kitimat. In keeping with Chinese customs, the Mah's celebrated the 'Full Moon' or the first month after birth of their son. They invited many guests to the party, held in Nechako Lodge, the guesthouse of the Alcan.

In 1967, Bill Mah opened his own restaurant, the Chop Suey Kitchen, at 420 Enterprise Avenue. Since then, both husband and wife have been operating the restaurant with Bill working mainly in the kitchen and his wife managing the till. As the years went by, the couple had three more children. All the children were raised and educated in Kitimat. They are now grown up, each having earned a diploma or degree from post secondary institutes, living and working in either Vancouver and Toronto. When the children were young, no Chinese school was available to teach them their heritage and language. Gradually, they forgot their dialect and use only English to communicate with their parents.

The Mahs continue to work hard spending most of their time and energy in the restaurant as they have done since the beginning. Every day they start work at 4:00 pm and continue until midnight. At times, they feel tired, but their children are not interested in carrying on the business.

"I won't blame them for not wanting to run a restaurant business. It is a hard life and time consuming," said Bill Mah. "You know, we Chinese parents always want to provide the best education to our children, hoping that they will be equipped with skills to face the challenges of life. Therefore we seldom suggest to them that they should continue with the restaurant business. Instead we encourage them to learn a skill or study for a profession."

Since they have spent so much time in the restaurant and in raising their family, they have little time to participate in any activities in the community. They have not even observed the most important Chinese festival, Chinese New Year.

"In the past, we were so busy making a living that we did not know Chinese New Year had arrived," said Bill Mah. "Our restaurant remained open during Chinese New Year, and we did not have time to celebrate the festival. But we closed the restaurant for a couple of days at Christmas and therefore we celebrated Christmas instead. We have more or less become 'lo fan'." Lo fan is a Cantonese term meaning "old foreigners". The term, in effect, refers to white Canadians as well.

Hing C. Mung and other Chinese Employees in Alcan

Many people have credited the development of Kitimat to the Alcan Company because of the jobs it created in the community, helping the population in Kitimat to increase. Later, other industries, such as the Eurocan Paper and Pulp and the Methanex/Pacific Ammonia, established their plants in the area. Although Kitimat can be reached by road, water and air the place is still isolated. Many qualified tradesmen stayed in Kitimat for a short period and then left town when they could find employment in less remote areas. Hence, Alcan often experienced the problems of tradesmen turnover, particularly in the early 1970s, and active recruitment of skilled personnel became necessary. Job positions were advertised in Hong Kong, Taiwan and Southeast Asia to attract men with skills to work in the Alcan Smelters. Trade transactions had already begun between Kitimat and Hong Kong. The first cargo of 123 tons of aluminum was shipped from Vancouver to Kowloon, Hong Kong on the January 11, 1955.[4] The metal was to be used for manufacturing aluminum cooking utensils, thus Alcan became familiar to people in Hong Kong. When the job positions were advertised in Hong Kong, a number of qualified tradesmen applied for the positions. Alcan agreed to assist the successful candidates in applying for visa and landed immigrant status in

Hing Mung, president of Alcan Asia
Limited, Hong Kong.

Photo courtesy Alcan Smelters Ltd.

Canada. It was indeed a good opportunity for qualified people to emigrate from Hong Kong.

In 1970, Hing C. Mung from Hong Kong joined the Alcan Company as a millwright in the Kitimat smelter. Over the years he worked hard and advanced to the position of President of Alcan Asia Ltd. in Hong Kong.

"I initially joined Alcan because it was recognized as a reputable company. I saw the chance for a better growth and advancement of my career with this company," said Mung.

In 1974 he went to Hong Kong and recruited tradesmen on behalf of the Alcan Smelters, and he encouraged many of his friends and classmates in Hong Kong to join the company in Kitimat. The recruitment provided opportunities for a good number of professionals and tradesmen. It also helped the Alcan Smelters to maintain its work force. Since then the recruitment of tradesmen from Hong Kong has become a tradition of the Alcan Smelters.

Prior to joining the Alcan Company, Mung was a qualified tradesman in a shipping company in Hong Kong. After working in the smelter for a year, he took a leave of absence and went to the University of Alberta. In 1976, he obtained a Bachelor of Science in Mechanical Engineering. While he was studying, he returned to work in the smelter every summer. After his graduation he rejoined the company as an engineer. One summer, he met Cecilia Chow, the youngest sister of Mrs. Lena Wong, at a banquet in Gim's Restaurant in Terrace. At that time, Chow, a qualified nurse from Hong Kong, was working at the Mill's Memorial Hospital in Terrace. They fell in love and got married. Later, the couple had a son, Alex.

Mung was soon promoted to the position of engineering manager. Between 1987 and 1992, he was the general manager of the Alcan Joint Venture in Shenzhen, one of the special economic zones in China. He also took charge of management and production. In 1992, he was appointed as President of Alcan Nikkei China Ltd. He then went to Harvard University where he graduated from the Harvard Business School Advanced Management Program. In 1995, he became the Vice President of Alcan Asia Pacific Ltd., responsible for the management of field projects. He also looked after corporate and general affairs, joint ventures and international trade and finances in Southeast Asia and China. Soon, he was promoted to the position of President of Alcan Asia Ltd. His office in Hong Kong is the headquarters for marketing and sales of Alcan Groups' products to Southeast Asia, China and in other Asia Pacific countries.

On the international stage, Mung is a director of Nippon Light Metal Company Ltd. and an executive director of the Nonfemet International Aluminum Company Ltd. He is the past Governor of the Canadian Chamber of Commerce, Hong Kong, and a member of the Professional Engineering Association of British Columbia. As an executive of the Alcan Company, he often travels throughout Canada, the United States, the United Kingdom and different countries in Southeast Asia to meet with other executives, and to hold seminars and conferences. In the midst of his busy schedule he usually takes time to visit his relatives and friends in Terrace and Kitimat whenever he comes back to British Columbia.

Lo Kin Ming, Tam Ka Chung and Lai Tung Hoi are a few of the recruits from Hong Kong among more than thirty Chinese workers in the Alcan Smelter. They came at different time periods, though, and each of them had his reason for joining the Alcan Company.

"In 1974, Hing Mung came to Hong Kong to recruit tradesmen. I knew him, as he was my senior in trade school. He encouraged a few of us to apply," said Lo Kin Ming, a millwright in the smelter. "I sent in my application, sat for a test designed by Alcan, and went through the interview process. I was lucky to get selected. Thus I came to Canada as a landed immigrant,"

Lo was a bachelor when he first arrived in Kitimat. Two years later he went back to Hong Kong to marry Rosita and returned with her to Kitimat. Lo feels that it is a good opportunity for him to work in a foreign company and see other parts of the world. Although he has lived in Hong Kong, a hustle and bustle metropolis, he prefers the quiet and peaceful environment of Kitimat.

Tam Ka Chung from Hong Kong went through a similar recruitment procedure when he joined the company.

"In 1980, I met a former classmate in Hong Kong who was working at the Kitimat smelter. He told me there were vacancies in the smelter and recommended that I apply. I sent in my application, sat for the Alcan test and obtained a job as a mechanic at the Kitimat smelter," said Tam Ka Chung.

Tam came because he wanted to live in a politically stable country. In the eighties every one knew that Hong Kong would return to the People's Republic of China even though official negotiations between China and Britain had not begun. Some people did not have confidence in the Communist regime, especially after the Cultural Revolution, and wanted to leave Hong Kong as soon as possible. Since North America is an attractive place for people in China, Southeast Asia, Hong Kong and Taiwan to live, many Asians dream of immigrating to either the United States or Canada.

"When I was in Hong Kong I had the chance to observe some actions or agitation of the leftists. They were quite disturbing and alarming at times," continued Tam. "Also being able to get a job overseas raises one's self-esteem and pride. It makes one feel good and lucky to have the opportunity to work for a reputable company in Canada. These factors helped me decide to emigrate from Hong Kong."

Just before he immigrated, Tam married Anita, and together they came to Canada. After a few years of their marriage, two daughters were added to the family. These two teenagers are aquatic athletes who have represented Kitimat in swimming competitions throughout BC.

Similarly, Lai Tung Hoi went through the application procedure and was successful in getting employment in the Alcan Smelters. He and his wife then emigrated to Kitimat.

"At the beginning I was not sure if I wanted to come and work at the Alcan Smelters," said Lai. "I did not know if I could adjust and live in a western country. But after I succeeded in getting the job, I felt obliged to give myself a chance, working in Canada. I am glad I made that decision because life has been pleasant and agreeable for my family."

However, not all the Chinese Canadians in the Alcan Smelters came from Hong Kong. Some came from Taiwan, Singapore, Malaysia and China, Harry Cheng among them. In November 1969, Cheng came from Taiwan as a landed immigrant and arrived in Vancouver. He stayed there for a short while, then went to the United States to further his studies in metal processing. In 1973, Harry Cheng joined Alcan. Currently, he is a process control supervisor in the plant.

"In the sixties and seventies, many young graduates from high schools, colleges and universities in Taiwan and Southeast Asia, hoped and dreamed to go abroad for further studies. It was a common trend in those days that young scholars went overseas to continue their education in universities or to carry out research in their specialty. I was no exception. After two years of studying in the States, I joined the Alcan Company here," said Cheng.

In 1988 Pang Wei Ming, an electrical engineer, came from Singapore with his wife Cai Ting Yun. Pang worked at Kemano until 1993 before he joined the Alcan Smelters in Kitimat. Over the past 10 years their family has grown to include three children. Interested in education, Pang became involved with the local school board and was elected as a school trustee of School District 80 in 1996.

"My husband got involved in the school board because he wanted to know more about the education system in this province," said Cai. "It was a good experience for him. However, when the School District amalgamated with other districts to form School District 82 he retired from his position." Cai paused and then continued, "We have a young family. As a school trustee he had many responsibilities. Public life took too much of his time from the family and we truly missed him. He, too, missed the children and the opportunity of being involved in their activities."

Unlike the first settlers, these capable and energetic Chinese Canadians have their families with them. Some of their wives are career women such as Gina Cheng and Anita Tam who work with Dr. Goschling, a dentist. Their children are going to school in Kitimat and some have graduated from high school. Oiman, the daughter of Lai Tung Hoi, is a graduate of the Kitimat Secondary School and continues her education at the University of British Columbia. Kevin, one of the sons of Harry and Gina Cheng, a grade 12 student also plans to go to university after graduation.

In general, most of the Chinese Canadians in Kitimat tend to dismiss the notion of prejudice and discrimination occurring in their community. "This is a relatively young community. There is no obvious segregation between those who came earlier and those who moved in during the last two or three decades. All of us, including the Caucasians in the community, are more or less on equal footing. Therefore, we have experienced very little racial disharmony," said Lo Kin Ming.

"Actually racism has many interpretations and depends on the perceptions of the people," commented Harry Cheng. "I am not saying that prejudice and discrimination are totally absent today. To me, racial discord occurs when people fail to communicate effectively. When people of different cultural backgrounds live together in a community, some misinterpretations of habits and behavior and some misunderstanding of customs and traditions are bound to occur. Therefore, it is important to promote understanding of one another's culture and to foster tolerance and acceptance of one another regardless of racial origins, color or creed."

The Chinese Employees in Eurocan

People in Kitimat and in the northwest region of BC have probably heard of Anthony Yao and his political activities. He is a specialist in the database-processing department in the Eurocan Paper and Pulp, which produces linerboard and other wood productions.

A history graduate of the Hong Kong Chinese University, Yao came to Canada as a foreign student in 1976. His original intention was to further his studies in history at the University of Western Ontario, but when he registered at the university, he changed his mind and went for an undergraduate program in computer science. Having completed a Bachelor of Science degree in 1979, he returned to Hong Kong and worked in the database-processing department of a shipping company. In 1981, he immigrated to Canada and joined the BC Rail Company in Vancouver, immediately starting work on the Tumbler Ridge Project. He worked for seven years at BC Rail in the database-processing department, and then he went to Vancouver Community College to obtain his diploma in Business Administration. In 1990 he joined Eurocan at Kitimat.

"I left Hong Kong because Canada had something very appealing to me. I was interested in Canada's heavy industries using its natural resources. I thought I would like to spend time learning and working in these industries," said Yao when asked why he came to Canada.

Being a bachelor, he has had time to volunteer his services to the community. In 1993, he was elected school trustee to serve on the School Board of School District 80 for three years. When the district amalgamated with other districts to form the Coast Mountains School Board 82, he was acclaimed as a school trustee in the new board.

Also, he is interested in provincial politics. His political inclination began when he was in the Hong Kong Chinese University where he had a professor from the United States who taught English history. This professor talked about the ideology of the Social Credit Party in England, which aroused Yao's interest. After being in Canada for a short while, he noticed that the Social Credit Party was active in British Columbia and Alberta.

"I was motivated to find out more about the Social Credit Party," said Yao. "I often wondered why a British political thought would flourish in British Columbia and Alberta. While I was at University of Western Ontario I spent a great deal of time studying the history and the mandate of the Socreds in Canada."

After studying and observing the Party for a number of years, he joined in 1993. He has been an active member and strong supporter of the Party, and has made great attempts to revive the Socreds. On June 9, 1998, he was elected as a second president of the Social Credit Party in BC.

Besides Yao, there are five other Chinese Canadians working in Eurocan. Wu Chi Hwa, a chemical analyst, is one of them. Wu and his family came to Canada from Brunei in 1980. He spent three years in Vancouver and then a number of years in Dawson Creek before he joined Eurocan in 1992.

The Chinese Employees in Methanex

Francis Huen is a chemist in Methanex/Pacific Ammonia's petro-chemical processing plant, which produces methanol, ammonia, de-icing chemicals and glues. This company sends its products to Japan and the United States. Huen emigrated from Hong Kong in 1974 and attended high school in Delta for two years. Then he went to the University of British Columbia, majoring in chemistry. In 1980, he graduated from UBC and carried out research on pesticides for two years at Simon Fraser University. In 1982, he joined Methanex, known as Ocelot at that time. His wife Elaine and daughter Emily are with him in Kitimat. He was the only Chinese employee in the Kitimat plant until the beginning of 1998 when Dr. Lu Gu Cai joined Methanex as a systems engineer.

The Chinese Community

The Chinese population in Kitimat increased in the seventies after Hing Mung took the initiative to recruit tradesmen from Hong Kong. Also, the other two large industries, Eurocan and Methanex, have attracted Chinese professionals and tradesmen to Kitimat. Since 1980 the number of Chinese Canadian and Chinese immigrant families has fluctuated between 35 and 40. Just like other Canadians, many Chinese skilled workers left town when they could find employment in less remote cities. Then the industries would recruit new employees from BC and Hong Kong. Other Chinese Canadians left town when they retired. For example, Dr. Chee Ling, a family practitioner, and his wife Joan left town a few years ago. He was a school trustee of School District 80 for two terms and served as a municipal councilor for three terms. Joan was also a school trustee of School District 80, and during her last term of office, she was chairperson of the board. Now both husband and wife are retired and living in Delta.

The number of Chinese residents in Kitimat may appear small but they are a group of progressive and vibrant Chinese Canadians. They have made great efforts to integrate into western society as well as retain their native language in the Chinese community while sharing their culture with others. They participate in Canada Day and multicultural events. During those events young children performed Chinese folk dances and sold exotic, homemade Chinese food in order to share their culture with other Canadians. The Kitimat Chinese also arrange on-going displays of Chinese arts, crafts and costumes.

Generally, they are pleased with the BC education system which focuses on the physical and mental development of a child as well as on the academic subjects.

"The Kitimat community gives us a sense of peace and security. It is good to bring up children in this kind of environment," said Gina Cheng. "Unlike the education systems in Hong Kong and Taiwan, which compel students to learn certain concepts before they are ready, our schools here allow our children to progress at their own speed. In this way, it has eliminated a lot of pressure on our children and has also given them a chance to develop their potentials and talents."

Chinese parents sometimes feel that it is a challenge to raise their children in western society. They have to deal not only with the generation gap but also with bridging cultural differences. Their children, as first generation Chinese Canadians, are exposed to the mainstream cultures with traditions, customs, values and beliefs, which are often different from those of a traditional Chinese family.

At times, young Chinese Canadians question the beliefs of their parents, not with the intention of undermining their parents' authority, but just wanting to know the rational behind such beliefs. The problem can be compounded if parents misinterpret their children's intention and do not realize that in Canada, children are taught to question anything they do not understand.

"Culturally speaking, I feel the younger generation is not quite as close to us as we would like them to be," commented Tam Ka Chung.

As loving and caring parents, they have shortened the cultural distance between generations through activities within the Chinese community. These activities focus on maintaining the Chinese culture and language for the younger generations, and developing bonds of friendship.

The Kitimat Chinese Canadian Association

About fifteen years ago, this group of energetic and conscientious parents formed a Chinese social club and christened it the Kitimat Chinese-Canadian Association.

"In this quiet little town we often visit one another and get together to play mahjong, especially in winter," said Gina Cheng. "On one occasion, some friends suggested forming a social club so that we would get to know each other. Although we had about thirty-five to forty Chinese families in the community, we seldom had the chance to meet one another. Also, new Chinese families kept arriving in town. It was near Chinese New Year, and two bachelors suggested celebrating Chinese New Year as a community and inviting the Lion Dance Troupe from Prince Rupert to perform. We took the initiative to go to every Chinese home to ask for donations, so that we would have funds to bring the Lion Dance Troupe to town and to rent the CAW Union Hall. That Chinese New Year celebration was a success. Almost all the Chinese Canadians in town turned up at the celebration, and many Chinese women prepared authentic Chinese New Year dishes for a potluck supper. After the celebration the suggestion of forming a Chinese club was again raised. Finally, we formed the club and elected our executive members."

The membership includes almost all the Chinese Canadians and immigrants from China, Hong Kong, Taiwan, Singapore, Malaysia and Brunei. In 1998 the executive members were Gina Cheng as President, Tam Ka Chung as Vice President, Wang Zhou as Secretary and Lo Kin Ming as Treasurer. Harry Cheng has served as a past president. It is a non-profit and apolitical organization whose objectives are to provide social functions for its members, share cultural activities with one another and promote Chinese heritage events in the Kitimat community at large. Members are required to pay a minimal membership fee every year. This money, along with funds from food and bake sales on Canada Day, is used to run the Association and to subsidize to their Chinese school. Since its formation, the Association has celebrated

Chinese New Year, Christmas, the Dragon Boat Festival and the Mid-Autumn Festival every year.

"During these occasions we explain the significance of the events to our children. We bring the events alive by telling the legends and stories behind the festivals. We hope that our children learn about their roots through these activities," said Lai Tung Hoi.

These stories and legends are deeply rooted in Chinese history. For example, one version of the Chinese New Year describes the struggles of some early Chinese farmers against a beast called *Nian* thousands of years ago. Apparently, *Nian* came out every winter and destroyed the farmers' properties, eating up their food and killing people. Eventually, the farmers succeeded in chasing the beast away by beating gongs and drums, and setting off firecrackers. Coincidentally, spring arrived after their victory. This is why Chinese New Year is known as *Guo Nian* meaning that their ancestors had overcome their struggles with *Nian*. Symbolically it also means leaving the past behind and welcoming the beginning of new life.

The Dragon Boat festival is an occasion to commemorate Qu Yuan, (屈原) a well known poet and statesman during the Warring States period (403 BC-211BC). Qu was born during the decline of the once powerful Kingdom of Chu. Qu's failure to win support from the corrupt Emperor and his court for his progressive proposals to reform the country made his life a tragic one. Seeing no future for his country, he drowned himself in Milo Jiang, a river in Hunan province. Fishermen nearby attempted to find his body but failed to retrieve it. Later on, the fishermen went out in their boats and threw rice wrapped in bamboo leaves to feed the fish in the river. They assumed the fish would not consume the body of Qu if they had something to eat.

This legend gradually evolved to become the Dragon Boat Festival involving a boat race either at a river or a lake. In China, Taiwan, Hong Kong, and Australia the dragon boat races have become an annual water sport. In this festival Chinese women prepare *zongzi*, steamed glutinous rice wrapped in bamboo leaves to commemorate Qu Yuan. As a politician Qu was a failure but as a poet he achieved great success. "*The Lament*" is one of his best poems, describing his feelings of oppression and frustrations.

When these stories are incorporated into the teaching of the Chinese language, they not only illustrate Chinese history but also the universal human spirit in its struggle to exist and its love for its country and fellow men.

"When we celebrate these festivals, we usually prepare and/or purchase traditional food and accôutrements for the occasion. For example, during Chinese New Year we give red packages, or lucky money, to our children and teach them how to express their appreciation in Chinese when they receive the gifts. They also have to say appropriate greetings such as Happy New Year or *xinnian kuale* to their elders and friends during the New Year. In this way we teach our children some Chinese customs and appropriate Chinese manners," said Gina Cheng.

"When we celebrate the Chinese festivals collectively, we provide our children the opportunity of getting together with one another as a group of young Chinese Canadians," said Tam Ka Chung. " our social club also holds two picnics in a year. We usually hold one picnic in June to observe the Dragon Boat Festival and another one in September to celebrate the Autumn Moon Festival. Through these activities our children have a chance to take part in some of our customs and traditions," remarked Tam Ka Chung.

"Frankly we are just trying our best," commented Harry Cheng. "To me, it is not right to forget our roots entirely. On the other hand it may not be practical for our children to hang on to all the Chinese values and beliefs. Don't forget our parents imparted their values and beliefs to us when we were in our home country. Now we are living in a different country. Some of what we inherited from our parents may not be appropriate or helpful to our children to live as Canadians. If we insist on holding our past, we may hinder or slow down our process of integration into the Canadian society. Now the question has become what aspects of the Chinese culture should we impart to our children, so that they can blend with other Canadian cultures and make their transition easier. We are only doing whatever possible to nurture our children and our heritage."

The Association represents a group of conscientious and progressive parents who want their children to benefit from the best of both worlds–Canadian and Chinese. Aware of their own limitations, the parents are attempting to fulfill the needs of their children living in a multicultural society. Some parents have expressed their concerns about the future of their children.

"Nowadays, it is common to find young graduates from university not being able to find a job," says Lai Tung Hoi. "In our time a certificate or a degree would guarantee a good paying job, but not now."

They also notice that the younger Chinese Canadians are somewhat isolated and have some difficulties fitting into the mainstream society because they are neither Chinese nor whites. To help these children to define their own identity, the parents have attempted to find ways of giving the children a sense of belonging. To achieve this and to ensure the children learn their heritage language, they established a Chinese school in 1994.

Nowadays, the young people often use English to communicate at home as well as in the community. This is natural because they attend public school where English is the language of instruction. Outside of their homes, they have to function in the English language. Gradually they tend to use English more than they use their native tongue. The Kitimat Chinese parents felt that setting up a Chinese school could help the young children to retain their heritage language, an important component of preserving any culture.

The Chinese School

In the beginning, a number of adults were involved in the teaching, including Gina Cheng and Cai Ting Yun. They used Mandarin or *Putonghua* as the medium of instruction since *Putonghua* is an official language of China. The teachers prepared their own teaching materials supplemented by those donated by the Taipei Trade and Economy Office and from the Consulate of the People's Republic of China in Vancouver. There were about twenty-five students including some parents and a two white Canadians. These students were grouped into three classes; one for young children ages between the ages of six and seven, one for students between eight and sixteen and one for parents. Many of the parents were from Hong Kong who could not speak *Putonghua*, and they wanted to learn how to speak the language with the correct tone and pronunciation.

"We hope to motivate our children to attend Chinese school by our presence," explained Anita Tam. "We adults know how to read and write Chinese characters but do not speak Mandarin well. Our purpose is to learn the correct pronunciation."

The classes were held in Kitimat Secondary School, where they were allowed to use the classrooms without charge. The intermediate group was held twice a week on Wednesday and Friday from 6:00 to 7:30 p.m. The primary group was held once a week on Friday from 6:00 to 7:30 p.m. After a year or so the adult class did not continue because there were no longer enough teachers to cover the three classes. Also, a couple of the parents did not continue due to other commitments. The difference in ages in the intermediate group also posed the greatest problems. The older students progressed faster than the younger ones. In fact, one teenager who spoke *Putonghua* at home found the lessons boring and meaningless. The younger students felt frustrated because they could not catch up with the older students; consequently, some of the teenagers dropped out. The white Canadian students also found the language too challenging and left the class.

After two years, the school was re-organized with Tam Ka Chung as the principal. The school used the Singapore Chinese Language Curriculum as a guideline for the teachers, bought textbooks, teaching materials such as exercises, and audio-video aids, which were part of the Singapore curriculum. In 1997-98 only twelve students remained in the two groups.

"I am not too concerned with the reduced number," said Tam Ka Chung. "Some of the older students have to leave because they are going to university or college. The intermediate group has changed to include children between the ages of twelve and sixteen only. It makes it less demanding for the teachers when the differences in age are smaller. Now we are educating a core of interested and motivated students. It is a healthy sign. Having a curriculum guide and appropriate teaching materials for the teachers has cut down the teachers' preparation time. Now that the school seems to be properly set up, I am sure it will prosper and attract more students in future."

Parents have to pay tuition for their children to attend the school. The money is used as an honorarium for the teachers. The administration in the Chinese Canadian Association recognize that the teachers spend time and effort in preparation as well as in teaching, so they agreed to give the teachers a token salary. The Chinese Association purchased the teaching aids and other supplies. Cai Ting Yun, one of the original teachers, still teaches the students in the intermediate group. In the meantime, Zhang He from China was recruited to teach the primary group. A mechanical engineer in China, she came to Kitimat with her husband and children in the mid 90s.

"I am not a teacher by profession. When I was in China I used to teach workers in a factory evening classes in mathematics and the Chinese language," said Zhang.

Both teachers are dedicated and employ a variety of teaching methods including games and singing in their instruction. They used *hanyu pinyin*, a pronunciation system, to teach the students the correct way to say things. They teach simplified Chinese characters, as these are the ones mainly used in China. Their teaching includes dictation, spelling, and reading comprehension for the older ones. During any festive season, they tell the students stories related to the occasion and include arts and crafts in their lessons. For example, during the spring festival they taught the students how to use a brush and ink to write out Chinese New Year greetings and sayings. In general, both of them are happy with the progress of their students.

"The primary class is relatively easy to teach because they are more or less of the same age group," said Zhang. "At the beginning I had some reservations since they were so young. Later, I discovered they did remember what was taught in previous classes. They love to play games and compete with one another. It is quite fun to teach them."

"The situation in the intermediate group is unique," commented Cai. "Some of the students speak Mandarin at home, and therefore we do not have a problem in communication. Other students from Hong Kong have difficulties in understanding spoken Mandarin or *Putonghua*. But, when I explained the words or phrases in Cantonese they picked up the concepts readily. Generally, they are learning well. I am pleased with their progress."

The Heritage Chinese School, indeed, has come a long way. The operation of the school has continued despite the difficulties and obstacles. The teachers and administration are determined to continue operating the school. Although the adult class is no longer in existence, the parents still support the school. Their Chinese Heritage School reveals the determination of this young Chinese community to retain their Chinese language and culture.

As indicated, the Chinese Canadians began to migrate to Kitimat in the seventies. Their history may be recent but is still significant. It illustrates the aspiration and hope of the Chinese Canadians in the community. They differ from the early Chinese immigrants who were usually single men involved in back-breaking menial labour that no one else wanted. When these recent immigrants came to Canada they had already made up their minds to make their homes permanently in this country. The early Chinese immigrants lived their lives as sojourners; they only wanted to find their fortune and then go home to spend the rest of their lives with their families. When this group of young Chinese immigrants arrived in this country, most of them already spoke enough English to communicate with all people in the community. The early Chinese immigrants were illiterate peasants, who had great difficulty in communicating with Caucasians. Their hopes and dreams were certainly different from the immigrants who came during the last four decades.

CONCLUSION

Throughout our Canadian history, prejudice and discrimination against immigrants of non-European descent has been prevalent and continues to this day. Though our ancestors were immigrants themselves, we somehow see ourselves as true Canadians and everyone else as invading our country to take our rights and privileges away from us. Being the modern and tolerant country that we continue to tell ourselves that we are, Canada advocates equal opportunity for its citizens and landed immigrants; we welcome everyone with open arms and make the world a better place. Yet the opportunity for newcomers to utilize their knowledge and expertise was and continues to be remote.

Indeed, it has always been a traumatic experience for immigrants coming to this country, as was the experience of the most recent immigration. Like the Chinese immigrants before 1940, they are regarded with fear and rejected by Canadian citizens.

During the process of settlement in Canada, past and present, the Chinese immigrants have gone through many trials and tribulations. Many experienced humiliation, rejection in their work fields–though they were qualified–as well as in their everyday life. Some Chinese Canadians and immigrants who are professionals still cannot find employment in this country. They live in uncertainty about their future as well as the future of their children. It is true that not all Canadians have treated immigrants badly, but it is important to point out that immigration to this country is still subject to racism and bias.

Throughout this book, the strength of conviction and perseverance of the Chinese immigrants shines through the hardships they had to endure. Some of them appear to have finally made it though that success was hard earned. Chinese people often say, "If you break open the silver we earn, you can see drops of blood in it." Indeed, how many people know the amount of tears the immigrants have shed and the number of sleepless nights they have spent while trying to make a living? It is truly fortunate that most Canadians have been kind and friendly to the Chinese Canadians in this region; otherwise life for them would have been completely unbearable and fulfilling their dreams would have been impossible.

CENSUS 1901 IN THE NORTHWEST

SKEENA AREA

Chinese Population

Ages	Number of Persons
1 - 19	29
20 - 29	198
30 - 39	157
40 - 49	104
50 - 70	60
	548 (total)

Chinese occupation

Cannery	373
Labour	46
Gold miner	41
Cook	32
Restaurant	2
Store keeper	2
Fishermen	2
Farmer	2
Chines store	1
House servant	1
Bookeeper	1
?	42
non-mentioned	3
	548 (total)

COAST DISTRICT AREA

Chinese Population

Ages	Number of Persons
1 - 19	5
20 - 29	18
30 - 39	10
40 - 49	3
50 - 70	5

41 (total)

Chinese occupation

Cook	14
Cannery	14
Labour	13

41 (total)

STIKINE AREA

Chinese Population

Ages	Number of Persons
1 - 19	0
20 - 29	0
30 - 39	13
40 - 49	10
50 - 70	19

42 (total)

Chinese occupation

Gold miner	35
Cook	3
Boat man	1
Domes	1
Not mentioned	2

42 (total)

Source: Canada Statistics

THE DESCRIPTION OF "FUSANG"
IN CHINESE LANGUAGE

梁書卷五十四

扶桑國者，齊永元元年，其國有沙門慧深來至荊州，說云：「扶桑在大漢國東二萬餘里，地在中國之東，其土多扶桑木，故以爲名。扶桑葉似桐，而初生如筍，國人食之，實如梨而赤，績其皮爲布以爲衣，亦以爲綿。作板屋。無城郭。有文字，以扶桑皮爲紙。無兵甲，不攻戰。其國法，有南北獄。若犯輕者入南獄，重罪者入北獄。在北獄者，男女相配，生男八歲爲奴，生女九歲爲婢。犯罪之身，至死不出。貴人有罪，國乃大會，坐罪人於坑，對之宴飲，分訣若死別焉。以灰繞之，其一重則一身屏退，二重則及子孫，三重則及七世。名國王爲乙祁，貴人第一者爲大對盧，第二者爲小對盧，第三者爲納咄沙。國王行有鼓角導從。其衣色隨年改易，甲乙年青，丙丁年赤，戊己年黃，庚辛年白，壬癸年黑。有牛角甚長，以角載物，至勝二十斛。有馬車、牛車、鹿車。國人養鹿，如中國畜牛。以乳爲酪。有桑梨，經年不壞。多蒲桃。其地無鐵有銅，不貴金銀。市無租估。其婚姻，壻往女家門外作屋，晨夕灑掃，經年而女不悅，即驅之，相悅乃成婚。婚禮大抵與中國同。親喪，七日不食，祖父母喪，五日不食，兄弟伯叔姑姊妹，三日不食。設靈爲神像，朝夕拜奠，不制縗絰。嗣王立，三年不視國事。其俗舊無佛法，宋大明二年，罽賓國嘗有比丘五人游行至其國，流通佛法、經像，教令出家，風俗遂改。」

八〇八

Source: Liang Shu, p. 808

~ 135 ~

BIBLIOGRAPHY

Books

Asante, N. *The History of Terrace*, Terrace Public Library Association, October, 1972.

Bays, H. Daniel, *China Enters the Twentieth Century*. Ann Arbor, the University of Michigan Press, 1978

Boyce, D. *Red, Yellow, White: Colours of the Salmon Canning Industry*, Questing, Archival Research & Creative Development, Victoria, 1997.

Blyth, Gladys Y. *Salmon Canneries, British Columbia North Coast*, Morris Printing Company Ltd., Victoria, BC 1991.

Bourgon, Nan, edited by Marjorie Rose Berge, *Rubber Boots for Dancing: memories of Pioneer life in the Bulkley Valley*, Tona and Janet Hetherington, Box 387, Smithers, BC

Bowman, P. *Klondike of the Skeena*, P. Bowman, 1700 Kootenay Ave., Prince Rupert, BC V8J 3S7. 1982.

P. Bowman, *City of Rainbows*, 1700 Kootenay Ave., Prince Rupert, BC V8J 3S7. 1982.

Chow, Lily, *Sojourners in the North*, Caitlin Press, Box 2387, Stn B Prince George, BC V2N 2S6, 1996

Harris, E.A. *Spokeshute: Skeena River Memory*, Orca Book Publishers, P.O. Box 5626, Stn B. Victoria, B, C. V8R 6S4, 1990.

Haig-Brown, Alan, *Fishing for a Living*, Harbour Publishing, Maderira Park, BC 1993

Laitinen, Kauko, *Chinese Nationalism in the late Qing Dynasty*, Scandinavian Institute of Asia Studies Monograph Series, No.57, Curzon Press, 1990.

Large. R.G. *Prince Rupert: A Gateway to Alaska and the Pacific*, Volume II, Mitchell Press, 1982

Skeena: River of Destiny. Gray's Publishing Ltd., Sidney, BC 1981

Lyons, Cicely, *Salmon: Our Heritage*, Mitchell Press Ltd., Vancouver, 1969.

Lee, T, H, David, *A History of Chinese in Canada*, [Chinese Version], Canadian Liberal Press, 1967

Leonard, Frank, *A Thousand Blunders*, UBC Press, Vancouver, 1996

MacKay, Donald, *The Asian Dream*, Douglas & McIntyre, Vancouver, BC 1986.

Meggs, G. *Salmon : The Decline of the British Columbia Fishery*, Douglas & McIntyre, Vancouver/Toronto, 1991.

Morton, J. *In the Sea of sterile Mountains: The Chinese in British Columbia.* J. J. Douglas, Vancouver, 1974.

Patterson, R. M. *Trail to the Interior*, William Sloane Associates Book, New York, 1966.

Roy, Patricia, *A White Man's Province : British Columbia Politicians and Chinese and Japanese Immigrants, 1858-1914*, University of British Columbia Press, Vancouver, 1989.

Shervill, Lynn, *Smithers: From Swamp to Village*, The Town of Smithers, Box 879, Smithers, BC V0J 2N0, 1981.

Turton, M. Conway, *Cassiar* The MacMillan Company of Canada, Toronto, 1934

Wicks, Walter, *Memories of The Skeena*, Hancock House Publishers Ltd., 3215 Island View Rd, Saanichton, BC V0S 1M0, Seattle, Washington 98168. 1976

Yao Xilian [Edited in Tang Dynasty] , *Liang Shu : Chinese History Anthology*, Volume III, Zhong Hua Press, Beijing, May 1973 [Chinese Version]

Journals

Appleyard, B. *Port Essington , B. C.: Whites and Indians*, The Mission Field, October 1,1897.

Ducker, James H. *Gold Rushers North, A Census study of the Yukon & Alaskan Gold Rushes, 1896 - 1900*, Pacific Northwest Quarterly, July 1994, p. 86

Godley, M. *The Sojourners*, Pacific Affairs, Volume 62, No.3, Fall, 1989.

Lee, David, *Chinese construction Workers on the Canadian Pacific Railway: Railroad History*, The Railway & Locomotive Historical Society, Vol/Issue: 148, 1981, p.42-57.

McCammon, Pat, *Bulkley Valley Stories : Mah Yak Tong*, Heritage Club
Project, Smithers, 1973.

Documents, Reports & Records

Aluminum Company of Canada Ltd., Facts About Kitimat & Kemano, BC
The Northern Sentinel Press, Kitimat, B. C. 1956

Asiatic & Oriental Immigration, 1909 - 1939, GR1547, Volume 474, B1132

British Columbia, County Court Record- Cassiar District - 1881 - 1892, GR
0580

British Columbia, County Court - Prince Rupert - 1908-1940 GR2527, Box
3, 4 & 5

British Columbia, County Court – Smithers – GR 2766, Gr 2867

Chock On Fond, 1928 -1940, Box 1 & 2, [Chinese Version] UBC Special
Collections.

Department of Fisheries, Correspondence & Applications for Licenses,
1907 -1910. Gr. 435, Box 14

Department of Mines, Miners Certificates in Cassiar District, 1879 - 1883.
Add MSS 646

Department of Mines, Mining Receipts in the Cassiar District, 1891 -1908.
Add MSS 649

Kitimat-Terrace Port Society, Kitimat-Terrace Port Project, Kitimat Marine
Terminal Development Prospectus, Vol.2 1991

Ledger of a Bakery in Smithers - Mah Yoke Tong - [Chinese Version],
Smithers, Archive and Museum, Special Collections, 1935 - 1950.

Lower, Joseph Arthur, *The Grand Trunk Pacific Railway*, [Thesis] University
of British Columbia, April, 1930 unpublished

Report of Canadian National Railways, Merger Agreement : Conductors,
Trainmen and Yardmen, 1929

Report of the Grand Trunk Pacific Commission, Session Papers No. 99,
May 17, 1924 (GR1972)

Report: North Pacific China House Archaeology Project, Shannon Mark &
Associates, NpCh 1992.

Ross, W.M. *Salmon cannery packs statistics : Nass & Skeena River of BC*
unpublished 1966.

Prince Rupert, British Columbia: the Pacific Coast Terminus of the Grand
Trunk Pacific Railway. The GTPR Company, Montreal, 1909, CIHM
74305

Prince Rupert Chinese Association : Constitutions and records of minutes, 1967, [Chinese version].

Prince Rupert Chinese Salvation Bureau, (hua qiao Jiu guo Hui) records of minutes, 1932 [Chinese version]

Prince Rupert, supreme Court Record, March 30, 1921

Vital Statistics 1900 – 1950, British Columbia Provincial Archives, Victoria.

Yip, Wayne Way, *The Chinese and Their Voluntary Associations in BC : A political machine interpretation*, Queen's University, Kingston, Ontario, November 1970 [unpublished thesis]

Newspaper and Magazine Articles.

Blyth, Gladys, "Meet Lee Wing, a Great Cook," *Prince Rupert Daily News*, August 8, 1987

Bowman, Phyllis, "Cunningham Built Port Essington As Base For Skeena River Travel," *Daily Colonist*, September 10, 1967.

Cox , Constancy, "Historic Hazelton has passed through Many Dangers," The *Province*, March 21, 1926, p.7 Magazine Section.

Culling, J. "Deus Lake Country May be Scene of New Gold Rush," The *Province*, January 24, 1923, Magazine Section.

Harris, Agnes, "The Ghosts Walk This BC Town, " The *Province*, May 3 1958, p.19

Leek, C. "The man behind the scenes" *Terrace Standard*, August 18, 1996

McKelvie, B. C. "Ancient Chinese Charm Relic of Early Migration to Coast," The *Province*, Sept 12, 1994, p.3

Newspapers:

Alcan Ingot, 1955 & 1997

Empire

Northern Sentinel, Kitimat 1971

Paper Clips, Eurocan Pulp and Paper Newspaper, Spring 1998

Port Essington Loyalist, Nov 7, 1907, January - August 1908.

Prince George Citizen

Prince Rupert Daily News

Smithers Interior News

Terrace Standard

Vancouver Province
Vancouver Sun
Vancouver World 1910 -1916
Victoria Daily Times
Victoria Daily Colonist

Magazines
Prince Rupert Travel Magazine, 1996.
Chinese Merchant Phone Directory, Vancouver, 1968-69
Growing with Prince Rupert, CN Rail, 1978.

Audio & Video Tapes
Orchard, Imbert, *People in landscapes : Growing up at the cannery*, CBC
    Interview Tape, 1978. No. 2498 - 1
People in landscape : Early Days of Commercial Fishing on the Skeena, CBC
    Interview tape 1978. No. 2455-1
The Parker Production, *The Cannery*, Video tape PMEC, Ministry of
    Education, BC 1987.

FOOTNOTES

Introduction

[1] Laitinen, <u>Chinese Nationalism in the late Qing dynasty</u>, SIAS, Curzon
   Press, 1978, p.39

[2] The *Vancouver Province*, January 1944, p.5 Magazine Section.

[3] Chow, <u>Sojourners in the North</u>, Caitlin Press 1996, p. 44 & 71

[4] The *Daily Colonist*, May 3, p.3; May 22, p.2, 1885.

[5] "Asiatic & Oriental immigrants 1907 –1939", GR 1547, Volume 474, B1132

[6] Godley, M. "The Sojourners," <u>Pacific Affairs</u>, Volume 62, No.3, Fall 1989

Chapter One

1 Cox, C. *Province*, March 21, 1926, p.7 Magazine Section.

2 Chow, <u>Sojourners in the North</u>, 1996 p. 99

3 Miner certificate index 14, GR 225, Volume 3

4 Roy, P. <u>A White Man's Province</u>, 1989, p.161

5 The *Province*, June 2, 1936, p.12; *The Daily Colonist*, June 3, 1936. P.5

6 Prince Rupert Supreme Court Record, March 30, 1921

Chapter Two

[1] Blyth, G.Y. <u>Salmon Canneries: British Columbia North Coast</u>, Oolichan
   Books, 1991 p.7

[2] Harris, E.A <u>Spokeshute</u>, Orca Publisher, 1990, p.143

[3] Orchard, Imbert, <u>People in Landscape</u>, CBC INTERVIEW Tapes, 1978,
   No. 2489-1

[4] Meggs, G. <u>Salmon: the Decline of the BC Fishery</u>, Douglas & McIntrye,
   Vancouver, 1991 p24

[5] Orchard, Imbert, <u>People in Landscape</u>, CBC Interview Tapes, 1978, No.
   2489 -1

[6] Wicks, W. <u>Memory of the Skeena</u>, Hancock House Publisher Ltd,
   Saanichaton, BC 1976 p.17-18
[7] Appleyard, B. "Port Essington, BC: Whites and Indians" <u>The Mission Field</u>,
   October 1, 1897 p.364
[8] Wicks W. <u>Memory of the Skeena</u>, Hancock House Publisher Ltd,
   Saanichaton, BC 1976 p. 17 -19
[9] Harris, E.A. <u>Spokeshute</u>, The Orca Publisher, 1990, p.133-134
[10] Harris, Agnes, "The Ghosts Walk in this BC Town" The *Vancouver
   Province*, May 3, 1958, p.19
[11] The *Vancouver Province*, July 5 1961 p.1

Chapter Three

[1] Cullins, J, "Dease Lake Country May be Scene of New Gold Rush," The
   Province, January 24, 1923.
[2] The *Daily Colonist*, October 21, 1882, p.3
[3] McKelvie, A. B. "Ancient Chinese Charm Relic of Early Migration to
   Coast," The *Province*, September 12, 1994, p.3
[4] Tang Yaosi, Edited, <u>Liang Shu : ancient Chinese anthology</u>, Zhonghua
   Shuju, May 1973, Volume 3 p.808
[5] Gold Commissioner's Casebook, 1878 to September 1982.
[6] The *Daily Colonist*, January 25, 1906, p.5: The *Province*, July 14, 1934, p.3
   Magazine Section.

Chapter Four

[1] The *Prince Rupert Daily News*, May 27, 1911 p.4 & June 10, 1911 p.1
[2] - ibid.- Nov 19, 1920 p.3
[3] BC county court, Prince Rupert, 1908 –1940, Gr 2527
[5] Large, <u>Prince Rupert</u>, Vol. II, Mitchell Press, 1982, p.40
[6] - ibid. – p. 42-44
[7] The *Prince Rupert Daily News*, October 22, 1980. p.15
[8] - ibid. -

[9] Mark S. *North Pacific China House :Archaeology Project*, 1992, p.3

[10] Lower, A. <u>The Grand Trunk Pacific Railway</u>, 1939. p.91

[11] MacKay, <u>The Asian Dream</u>, 1986, p 98-100; Roy, <u>White Man's Province</u>, 1989, p. 256 -257

[12] Railway Commission Report, Session Papers. No 99, May 1924, GR 1972

Chapter Five

[1] Yip, <u>The Chinese and their Voluntary Association in B. C.</u> Queen's University, Kingston, Ontario, Thesis, [unpublished] November, 1970, p.33

[2] The *Prince Rupert Daily News*, June 25, 1971. P.2

[3] The *Sun*, June 16, & 18, 1960 p. 8 & p.4 respectively

Chapter Six

[1] Asante, N. <u>The History of Terrace</u>, 1972, p 183

[2] Vital Statistics, British Columbia Provincial Archives

[3] Godley, M.R. " *The Sojourners: Returned Overseas Chinese in the People's Republic of China*," <u>Pacific Affairs</u>, Volume 62 No.3 Fall 1989

[4] Leykauf, C. "The man behind the scenes," The *Terrace Standard*, August 28, 1996 p. B1

Chapter 7

[1] Shervill, <u>Smithers: From Swamps to Village</u>, 1981, p.10

[2] Smithers county court, GR 0580, Gr. 2766, Gr. 2867

[3] Shervill, <u>Smithers: From Swamps to Village</u>, 1981, p.10

[4] Leonard, K. <u>One Thousand Blunders</u>, UBC Press, Vancouver, 1996, p.107

[5] McCammon, "*Mah Yoke Tong*", 1973, p 133

Chapter 8

[1] Aluminum Company of Canada Ltd. "Facts About Kitimat & Kemano, BC" The Northern Sentinel Press, Kitimat, B. C. 1956, p.5

[2] -Ibid. - p.4

[3] The *Sun*, July 25, 1951, p.1

[4] The *Alcan Ingot*, Jan 1955, p.4

INDEX

INDEX